Social Media Marketing

Social Media Marketing

Strategies in Utilizing Consumer-Generated Content

Emi Moriuchi

BEP BUSINESS EXPERT PRESS

Social Media Marketing: Strategies in Utilizing Consumer-Generated Content

First published in 2016 by
Business Expert Press, LLC
222 East 46th Street, New York, NY 10017
www.businessexpertpress.com

ISBN-13: 978-1-63157-118-3 (paperback)
ISBN-13: 978-1-63157-119-0 (e-book)

Business Expert Press Digital and Social Media Marketing and Advertising Collection

Collection ISSN: 2333-8822 (print)
Collection ISSN: 2333-8830 (electronic)

Cover and interior design by Exeter Premedia Services Private Ltd., Chennai, India

First edition: 2016

10 9 8 7 6 5 4 3 2 1

Printed in the United States of America.

Abstract

With the introduction of the Internet, consumers have been relying heavily on the media for content. The popularity of consumer-generated content (CGC) has captured the consumer (i.e., user) as the producer, which has caused a power shift in the market from companies to consumers. When technology is paired with culture, it is inevitable that consumers constantly change their attitudes toward consumption to adapt to current trends. Thus, marketers are meticulously looking for information to stay current with the consumer market in order to maintain their market share. CGC is closely related to electronic word-of-mouth (eWOM) and is found on various online review sites, forums, blogs, company websites, and social media platforms. Consumers' contribution toward the content on different digital media sites (including a company's website) is voluntary, either paid (e.g., sponsored) or nonpaid (e.g., personal blogs). It is evident that information that is published online travels faster to consumers than when delivered through traditional media such as television. Thus, companies are trying to be proactive and, as a part of their promotional efforts, are turning to online media for the latest information on their target market, feedback on their company (e.g., criticism, praises), and information on their competitors. However, despite the convenience of knowledge transfer via the Internet, there are still disadvantages of the use of CGC. The goal of this book is to educate business owners, marketing practitioners, students, and marketing researchers about the use of CGC and how it is beneficial for their marketing plan.

Keywords

consumer behavior, consumer decision-making, consumer-generated content, content marketing, cross-national, culture, marketing communication, process, social media, storytelling

Contents

Preface

Is our life getting more convenient and more complex at the same time? Research shows that with social media taking the consumer market by storm, companies no longer have the option to stay out of the virtual community. As the power shifts from companies to consumer, companies are scrambling to find means and ways to retain as well as capture new customers. How else should companies know what consumers want? The answer is to listen.

Consumer-generated content (CGC) largely occurs on new media and this new media is a paradigm shift in social media marketing. Although the Internet allows direct communication between consumers and consumers or businesses and consumers (or both), the amount of exposure (e.g., online ads) is not necessarily voluntary for consumers. With the birth of social media, consumers are now in control of what they want to see and what they want to use as valuable information in their decision-making process (e.g., purchase intentions).

The purpose of this book is to organize and clarify key information about CGC. This information is intended to benefit small business owners, marketing practitioners, students, and marketing researchers in understanding the use of CGC as part of a marketing plan.

We begin the book by defining the term CGC. CGC is often linked to electronic word-of-mouth (eWOM) as well as to social media. We next discuss the role of consumers as CGC contributors and the changing landscape of marketing communications.

We also review the different forms of CGC (e.g., reviews, blogs, and collaborative content), in addition to looking at why CGC is so popular in the consumer market; specifically, we examine the core characteristics of CGC. The consumer's motivation to contribute to CGC is also an important element of this book. Since CGC is deemed to be more credible than company-published content, we want to understand how and why companies can motivate their target consumers to contribute to CGC.

In order to look at CGC from a global perspective, three countries were selected, on the basis of their cultural orientations and acceptance toward social media: the United States of America, Japan, and Singapore. The United States, known to be the first mover in major social media, is generally populated with individualistic consumers, whereas Japanese consumers are commonly categorized as collectivistic. Singaporean consumers are often considered bicultural. They may be of Asian descent but their cultural orientation is fairly westernized. The book focuses on how these different types of consumers adapt toward social media and their willingness to engage in CGC.

With the large amounts of information posted online, how do we know which information to trust? This book will focus on trust on CGC. In addition, we adopt a case to exemplify consumers' opinion about using certain platforms. Research demonstrates that CGC has a great impact on the consumer market. Companies are thus faced with both opportunities and challenges when dealing with CGCs either on their corporate website or on a social media site.

Last but not the least, we present an overview of the future of CGC, the positive and negatives of CGC as well as opportunities for marketers. This book should benefit and share useful information to a broad audience, including marketing practitioners, students, and professors teaching marketing. This book is also a concise read for business managers interested in promoting their business using CGC (maybe even a norm now) with new social media tools.

Acknowledgments

I would like to thank the publisher, Business Expert Press, for giving me this opportunity to express my interest in this book. I would also like to extend my gratitude toward my editor, Dr. Vicky L. Crittenden, for giving me constructive feedback for continuous improvements.

Last but not the least, I would like to thank my family members. Thanks to my brother for the Singapore piece in this book. Mom and Dad, thank you for being so understanding. Thank you Tse, for your continuous support, and Kyler for letting mommy write.

CHAPTER 1

What Is Consumer-Generated Content?

With the introduction of the Internet, individuals have become increasingly dependent on their mobile devices as these devices give them access to the digital world in seconds. Regardless of whether consumers are trying to obtain, accept, or deliver information, or simply just searching for it, they are relying on the digital environment as their source for information.

The importance of consumer-generated content (CGC) has increased over that of companies' self-published content in the online world. This suggests that online information has shifted from publisher-centric to consumer-centric. CGC, as suggested by the name, is driven by consumers. Consumers create or produce (or both) any type of content (e.g., reviews, videos, photos, etc.) and share it with the general public. The channel of distribution is primarily the Internet. With innovative means of communication, the potential for a company to reach its mass audience is high. With Web 2.0 technologies, websites are given more support with the creation and consumption of CGC. Some of these CGC platforms include YouTube, MySpace, Facebook, Wikipedia, blogs, and community forums. The advent of Web 2.0 technologies has offered CGC a large opportunity to target its niche market within the media landscape, which attracts "more than $450 million" in advertising revenue (Verna 2007).

In a technologically advanced society, consumers are gaining more control over their decision-making processes and the amount of media exposure that they want to experience. As the conventional media model becomes obsolete, researchers are trying to understand consumers' motivational factors that drive them to go online to look for information. Severin and Tankard (1992) argued that due to this power shift, media theorists are changing their audience identification process by focusing on understanding why and how consumers use media rather than the theoretical effects of media on these audiences. This suggests that CGC has a strong impact on the media environment, which indicates the importance of understanding the motivation of consumers and creators behind creating and contributing such media content. As consumers around the world adapt to the use of the Internet, communication channels are gradually increasing, creating a better and smoother flow of communication between consumer-to-consumer (C2C) as well as business-to-consumer (B2C).

By definition, CGC refers to materials that are created and uploaded to any Internet sites by nonprofessionals (www.iab.net). This also means that the content is not contributed by an expert, but rather by a consumer who has first-hand experience with a product or service. With the introduction of high-speed Internet and search engines, CGC has become one of the prevalent forms of global media. In fact, it is one of the fastest growing commodities on the Internet. According to a platform status report by Interactive Advertising Bureau (IAB) (2008), in the year 2006, CGC attracted 69 million users in the United States alone. With such a large user population, the revenue of $1 billion in advertising in 2007 proved that CGC is a dynamic new medium in this new future.

In general, CGC focuses on product reviews and restaurant services especially for airline companies, cell phone services, restaurants, hotels, and resorts. Ye et al. (2011) and others (Hu and Liu 2004) noticed that the amount of CGC contributed online is extensive, to a point where companies pay CGC writers to contribute reviews on their company website or sites that have the company name mentioned (e.g., Yelp!). Some may think that online reviews do not have considerable impact on the sales of a product or the percentage of patronage from a customer. This assumption is definitely incorrect. CGC has proven to be extremely influential and it has the ability to fold a business.

From Wikipedia and blogs to Facebook, various information is spread across different Web 2.0 outlets. All these outlets are known as CGC or sometimes known as user-generated content. CGC is a more commercial label that demands more "nuanced, innovative, and exotic methodologies" (Hardey 2011, p. 13). Consumers are constantly retrieving instant information with the click of a button. As consumers gain power over the consumer market, companies are redefining their market reach, frequency, and consumer targeting. Social media has definitely taken a leap in capturing the intended audiences and building brand relationships. It has long overtaken the traditional, product-driven, one-way street in marketing communication. Moreover, the introduction of social media has adopted the approach of new information and consumer-driven objectives.

In the past, CGC platforms were users' sources to gain information from their peers. In 1980, a platform known as Usenet, a computer network communication system, was established. This was the oldest communication system before the birth of the World Wide Web (WWW). Usenet works fairly similarly with the current social media platforms, just on a smaller scale. For example, when a user posts an article, it is initially available on his or her news server. This news server will then talk to one or more servers and exchange articles with them. On Usenet, it is normally the sender rather than the receiver who initiates the transfer. These articles were treated as bulletin boards known as "newsgroups." On these newsgroups, only text was displayed. Unlike the sophisticated platforms nowadays with videos and photos, Usenet contained discussions based solely on the text that was shared. Many Usenet users would argue that it was the only genuine "space" people could publicly share information with unclear ownership. One of the best aspects of Usenet was that it was the only platform that "encouraged thoughtful, long-form writing with lots of quotation and back-and-forth" (www.pcmag.com). Social media has evolved over time and what used to be the trend is now outshined by new social media platforms. Figure 1.1 shows the timeline of the various consumer-generated platforms in social media.

Before discussing the motivation behind consumers' consumption, participation, and production of CGC, we will first define the meaning of "consumer," "content," and "e-commerce" in the online marketing context.

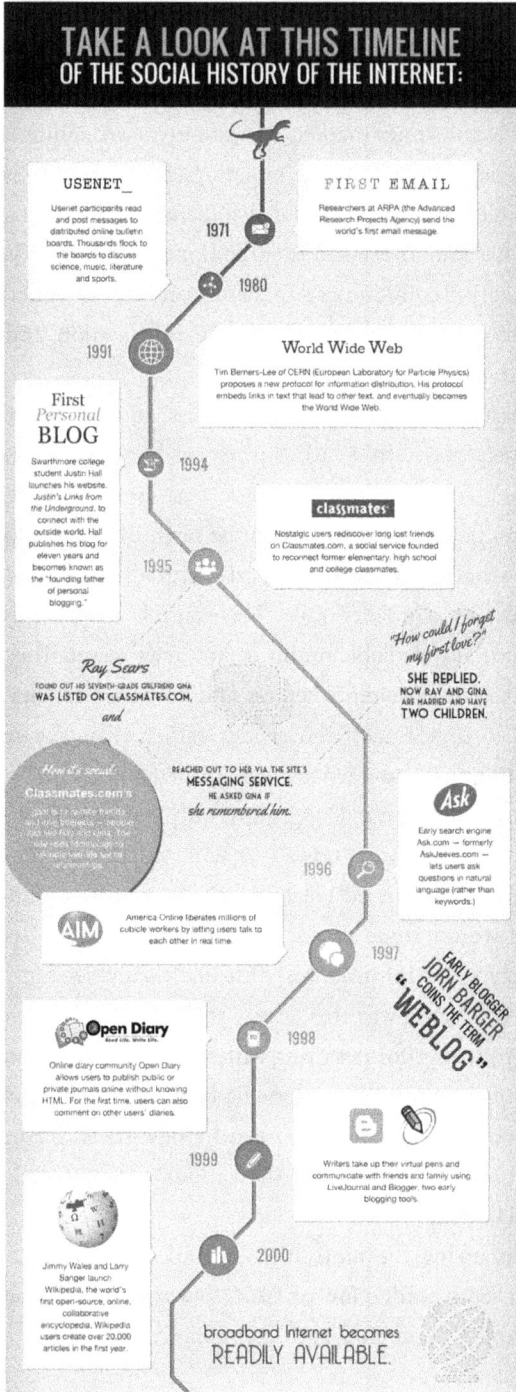

TAKE A LOOK AT THIS TIMELINE
OF THE SOCIAL HISTORY OF THE INTERNET:

USENET_

Usenet participants read and post messages to distributed online bulletin boards. Thousands flock to the boards to discuss science, music, literature and sports.

FIRST EMAIL

Researchers at ARPA (the Advanced Research Projects Agency) send the world's first email message.

1971

1980

1991

World Wide Web

Tim Berners-Lee of CERN (European Laboratory for Particle Physics) proposes a new protocol for information distribution. His protocol embeds links in text that lead to other text, and eventually becomes the World Wide Web.

First *Personal* BLOG

Swarthmore college student Justin Hall launches his website, *Justin's Links from the Underground*, to connect with the outside world. Hall publishes his blog for eleven years and becomes known as the "founding father of personal blogging."

1994

classmates

Nostalgic users rediscover long lost friends on Classmates.com, a social service founded to reconnect former elementary, high school and college classmates.

1995

"How could I forget my first love?"

Ray Sears

FOUND OUT HIS SEVENTH-GRADE GIRLFRIEND GINA WAS LISTED ON CLASSMATES.COM, *and*

SHE REPLIED. NOW RAY AND GINA ARE MARRIED AND HAVE **TWO CHILDREN.**

How it's social

Classmates.com's

REACHED OUT TO HER VIA THE SITE'S **MESSAGING SERVICE.** HE ASKED GINA IF *she remembered him.*

Ask

Early search engine Ask.com — formerly AskJeeves.com — lets users ask questions in natural language (rather than keywords.)

1996

AIM

America Online liberates millions of cubicle workers by letting users talk to each other in real time.

1997

EARLY BLOGGER **JORN BARGER** COINS THE TERM **"WEBLOG"**

Open Diary

Online diary community Open Diary allows users to publish public or private journals online without knowing HTML. For the first time, users can also comment on other users' diaries.

1998

1999

Writers take up their virtual pens and communicate with friends and family using LiveJournal and Blogger, two early blogging tools.

2000

Jimmy Wales and Larry Sanger launch Wikipedia, the world's first open-source, online, collaborative encyclopedia. Wikipedia users create over 20,000 articles in the first year.

broadband Internet becomes **READILY AVAILABLE.**

(Continued)

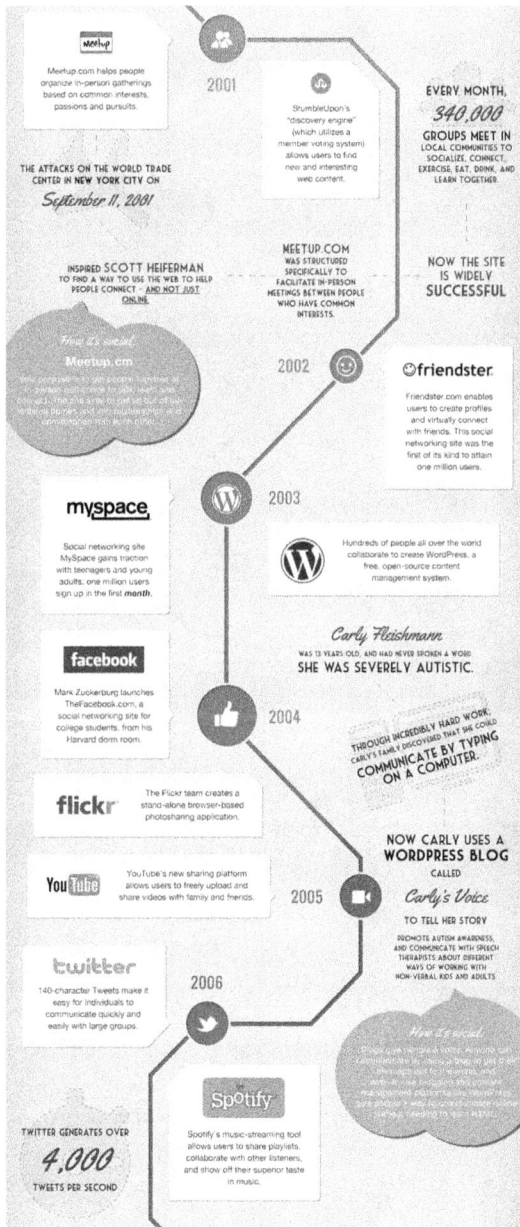

Meetup.com helps people organize in-person gatherings based on common interests, passions and pursuits.

2001

StumbleUpon's "discovery engine" (which utilizes a member voting system) allows users to find new and interesting web content.

EVERY MONTH,
340,000
GROUPS MEET IN LOCAL COMMUNITIES TO SOCIALIZE, CONNECT, EXERCISE, EAT, DRINK, AND LEARN TOGETHER.

THE ATTACKS ON THE WORLD TRADE CENTER IN NEW YORK CITY ON
September 11, 2001

INSPIRED SCOTT HEIFERMAN TO FIND A WAY TO USE THE WEB TO HELP PEOPLE CONNECT – AND NOT JUST ONLINE.

MEETUP.COM WAS STRUCTURED SPECIFICALLY TO FACILITATE IN-PERSON MEETINGS BETWEEN PEOPLE WHO HAVE COMMON INTERESTS.

NOW THE SITE IS WIDELY SUCCESSFUL

How it's social.
Meetup.cm

2002

friendster
Friendster.com enables users to create profiles and virtually connect with friends. This social networking site was the first of its kind to attain one million users.

myspace
Social networking site MySpace gains traction with teenagers and young adults. one million users sign up in the first *month*.

2003

W
Hundreds of people all over the world collaborate to create WordPress, a free, open-source content management system.

facebook
Mark Zuckerburg launches TheFacebook.com, a social networking site for college students, from his Harvard dorm room.

Carly Fleishmann
WAS 13 YEARS OLD, AND HAD NEVER SPOKEN A WORD.
SHE WAS SEVERELY AUTISTIC.

2004

THOUGH INCREDIBLY HARD WORK, CARLY'S FAMILY DISCOVERED THAT SHE COULD COMMUNICATE BY TYPING ON A COMPUTER.

flickr
The Flickr team creates a stand-alone browser-based photosharing application.

NOW CARLY USES A
WORDPRESS BLOG
CALLED
Carly's Voice
TO TELL HER STORY

You Tube
YouTube's new sharing platform allows users to freely upload and share videos with family and friends.

2005

PROMOTE AUTISM AWARENESS, AND COMMUNICATE WITH SPEECH THERAPISTS ABOUT DIFFERENT WAYS OF WORKING WITH NON-VERBAL KIDS AND ADULTS

twitter
140-character Tweets make it easy for individuals to communicate quickly and easily with large groups.

2006

How it's social.

TWITTER GENERATES OVER
4,000
TWEETS PER SECOND

Spotify
Spotify's music-streaming tool allows users to share playlists, collaborate with other listeners, and show off their superior taste in music.

(Continued)

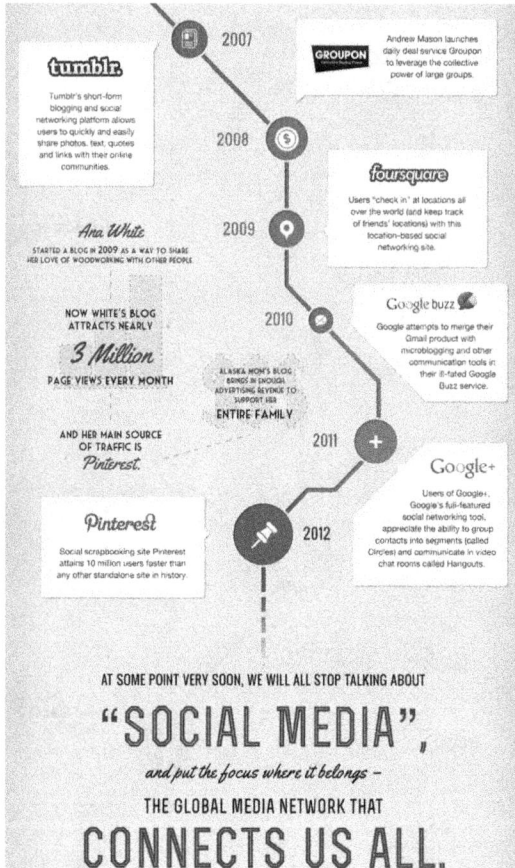

Figure 1.1 The timeline of social media

Source: Hayden and Tomal (2012).
Permission to use image was sought and attained from CopyBlogger.

Definition of "Consumer"

The term "consumer" refers to the primarily consumers themselves—anyone other than professional writers, journalists, and publishers. The communication messages posted by CGC consumers are often anonymous (Campbell et al. 2011), whereas word-of-mouth (WOM) communicators are often "known to each other or at least identifiable" (p. 89). Stern (1994) defines WOM as the "utterances that are personally motivated, spontaneous, ephemeral, and informal in structure—and are not paid by sponsors" (p. 89). Nonetheless, there has still been a debate over whether WOM is more reliable than CGC. Skeptics argue that rational consumers doubt the credibility of the anonymous comments on CGC and still value online WOM (Mayzlin 2006). Campbell et al. (2011) argued that though CGC and eWOM have similar traits, communication of these two forms still differs in certain ways. On the other hand, Wang and Rodgers (2010) view eWOM as a type of online advertising that uses CGC platforms. They argue that eWOM is a specific type of CGC that is a critical component of marketing as consumer-generated reviews are regarded as more credible and less biased (Keller 2007).

Lastowka (2007) defined "user" as a dichotomy between "those who make things and those who use them" (p. 899). When the term CGC is used in the consumer market, a "user" is often aligned with other possible connotations such as consumers, purchasers, and audiences. Thus, in order to have a consumer produce CGC, there should be technology. In other words, the term CGC implies that there is an existence of two parties (producers and consumers) and two things (communication tools and content). In the context of this digitalized consumer market, the two parties will be the CGC producers and CGC consumers and the two possible artifacts will be social media platforms and product reviews.

Generally, consumers comprise the public at large. For many companies, CGC is often described as a benefit to both businesses and a type of grassroots cultural revolution. In the past, content was generated professionally, whereas now, consumers are allowed to produce their own content with available communication tools such as social media sites. The contemporary interest in CGC may not be so much in the communication tools, but in how those who produce and distribute the content can own and profit other consumers using the Internet as a distribution platform.

Web 2.0 has provided amateur content creators an innovative way to produce content at a lesser cost, along with the ability to connect with others across great distances and to engage in entertaining one another through their words. These possibilities have changed the marketing communication landscape in the consumer market. Skeptics have been critical about the benefits of CGC for society (Campbell et al. 2011; Lastowka 2007). As content is shared among fellow consumers, the information provided may be criticized as amateurish. On the other hand, some may value the information provided by fellow consumers as it appears more honest and reliable compared to those generated by companies. In addition, such CGC may be a step toward improving traditional communication models of information production and distribution.

Definition of "Content"

The word "content" in CGC is used to describe relevant and valuable information that can be presented to an audience (Lastowka 2007). In the marketing field, more specifically in content marketing, the content that is created and distributed is focused on attracting and retaining a target audience, which ultimately drives profitable customer action (contentmarketinginstitute.com). Generally, this content is the message a company or consumer uses to communicate without selling. For example, if a consumer is planning a vacation, the content is relevant to the consumer's travel plans such as activities.

With the merging of Web 2.0 and CGC, content often comprises images, videos, or short messages posted on Instagram, YouTube, Facebook, and Twitter. Other content may also include book reviews, which may be posted on Amazon.com, and personal narratives posted on community forums and blogs. In the consumer market, consumer reviews are most significant for experiential products (Ye et al. 2011), especially when the quality of the product is unknown (Klein 1998). Litvin, Goldsmith, and Pan (2008) agreed that hospitality services are considered experiential products and are important sources of information for travelers (Pan, MacLaurin, and Crotts 2007). Furthermore, Gretzel, and Yoo (2008) recognized that travelers find reviews provided by fellow travelers are more up-to-date, enjoyable, and reliable compared to those provided by travel agencies.

According to Hayes (2015), CGCs such as photos, videos on social media, product reviews, and questions posted on the company website all play a "valuable role in creating a better shopping experience in today's digitally-driven environment" (para 1). Further, Hayes (2015) added that the most recognized content in CGC is online product reviews. She argued that this type of content gives consumers the freedom to share their experiences and knowledge of a product. On the other hand, it gives companies an edge as it helps brands better serve their customers.

Content is not only about consumers generating valuable information as a byproduct of their activities; content can also be data generated through search engines. Lastowka (2007) argued that consumer activities such as shopping online who unintentionally generates web-surfing histories (e.g., cookies). Lastowka (2007) claim that this is a form of understanding the fundamentals of CGC. This type of content is highly significant in terms of commercial value (Lastowka 2007, p. 896).

Definition of E-Commerce

CGC generally appears on the Internet through various communication channels. Consumers are assimilating into a web-based commercial information platform known as electronic commerce ("e-commerce") (Horrigan 2008). E-commerce activities such as online retailing and customer relationship management (CRM), have been fast growing domestically and globally and has been very competitive over the past decade (Fang et al. 2014). Transactions on this platform range from personal items to big box items such as furniture. According to the U.S. Census Bureau News (2015), sales generated from the U.S. retail e-commerce sector for the third quarter of 2015 was estimated at $81.1 billion. This is an estimated increase of 2.9 percent from the second quarter of 2015. The number of Americans who have purchased products online has also increased (pewresearch.com). Furthermore, according to GE Capital Retail Bank's second 2013 annual report (www.retailingtoday.com), 81 percent of consumers go online to gather information before heading out to the store. In fact, the number of consumers, either researching online or buying a product or service online, has nearly doubled (Horrigan 2008).

As the online retail industry has grown and become globally competitive over the past decade (Fang et al. 2014), online vendors are constantly being challenged with customer retention (Johnson, Sivadas, and Garbarino 2008). In e-commerce, CGC "may serve as a new form of WOM for products/services or their providers" (Ye et al. 2011, p. 635). For example, Duan, Gu, and Whinston (2008) found in their study that the valence of online consumer reviews had no significant impact on the box office's revenues. However, box office sales were significantly influenced by the volume of online reviews. In the tourism industry, however, Vermeulen and Seegers (2009) revealed that positive online reviews had an impact on the perception of hotels among their potential consumers. Regardless of whether it is the volume or valence of consumer reviews, such CGC has an impact on both the consumers and retailers (Zhu and Zhang 2006, 2010).

Within the virtual environment, several existing studies discuss influencing factors such as trust (Flanagin et al. 2014; Flavián, Guinalíu, and Gurrea 2006; Qureshi et al. 2009). This influencing factor is deemed a key predictor for customer retention because of its "crucial ability to promote risk-taking behavior in the case of uncertainty, interdependence, and fear of opportunism" (McKnight, Cummings, and Chervany 1998). However, Fang et al. (2014) realized that the impact of trust is not independent from its context. They proposed that investigating how trust operates under various different boundaries could help "specify regulative conditions" under which the effect of trust varies on online purchases (Gefen and Pavlou 2006). Practically, if firms are able to have a complete understanding of trust as a moderating effect on online purchases, they are able to "fine tune their online trust (re) production strategies" (Fang et al. 2014, p. 408).

Although trust is an essential factor for a hypercompetitive e-commerce environment, it is no longer the only triggering factor in customer's transaction intentions (Liu and Goodhue 2012). Building a trustworthy image is no longer an option; rather it is a necessity for ongoing operations for companies that have a virtual modality for transactions.

Thus, by having a good understanding of trust, online firms are able to allocate their "trust-building resources" (Fang et al. 2014) more cost effectively, thereby optimizing their return on investment by investing in trust production. A further discussion on trust is covered in Chapter 4.

The Changing Landscape of Marketing Communications

To meet the demand of a fast-paced lifestyle, the virtual world has changed its "laid-back" setting to a more complex and dynamic landscape comprising of both traditional and interactive media. Many companies that use traditional media such as TV or radio realize that they are struggling to provide an interactive environment that provides the opportunity to capitalize on this fragmented market. Companies attempt to offer their consumers a unique media channel (e.g., social media) that enables the latter to voice out among the rapid and enormous amount of information and advertisements (Daugherty et al. 2011).

Unlike mainstream traditional media such as television and radio, many consumers have moved toward an evolutionary change in lifestyle and toward the use of social media. With the abundance of "space" in the virtual world, online media has created a robust information hub for both marketers and consumers. The intention of creating this hub is to provide an efficient and timely communication channel. The challenge that companies currently face is the integration of their offerings with the lifestyle of those consumers. Anderson (2007) argued that despite the consistent growth of television viewership, television suffers from a production of program offerings that leads to fragmented audiences and a decline in program ratings. The Internet has reached a stage where it is the "go to" media outlet, above all other traditional media communication channels. According to the 2012 census bureau report, nearly 75 percent of American households use the Internet at home (www.census.gov). Furthermore, more than 78 percent of the adult population uses the Internet (www.census.gov).

Although consumers still utilize traditional media, the trends in media usage have changed drastically. Now, consumers have more control over what they want to use, hear, and see, and audiences are given the opportunity to create media content freely by themselves and not rely on traditional gatekeepers (e.g., publisher) (Perry 2002). Furthermore, research has indicated that the presence of the Internet has changed the way people communicate information. This communication process, known as WOM, is where consumers create, share, and propagate information (e.g. shopping experience) (Gupta and Harris 2010; Kozinets et al. 2010). Digitalized WOM (i.e., eWOM) is accessible 24 by 7 anywhere through diverse social media such as blogs, social networks, customer reviews, and forums, which has an impact on prospective or existing consumers (Dellarocas 2003; Schindler and Bickart 2005). It is not uncommon for a consumer to obtain information on a product from his friends or family. In addition, consumers can also expand their search effort by consulting fellow consumers' reviews, blogs that are specifically written on a particular topic or even summarized opinions contributed by micro-bloggers. According to Nielsen's Global Trust in Advertising Survey (2012), online consumer reviews are the second most trusted source for brand information—70 percent of global consumers attested to that claim. Earned media such as WOM or recommendations from family and friends, above all the other advertisements, was indicated as the most trustworthy source by 92 percent of the surveyed global consumers.

In the mid-1990s, companies were reliant on traditional business practices—marketing communication controlled by distinct and identifiable corporate spokespersons (Hoffman and Novak 1996). However, current marketing practices are "evolving into true participatory conversations" (Muñiz and Schau 2011, p. 209). Unlike in the past, marketing communications have transformed into two-way, many-to-many, multimodal communications. The impetus behind this dramatic change and the context in which these conversations are taking place is known as the Internet. Methods of marketing communication have been forced to adapt with the advent of the Internet and social media, for example, Facebook, Twitter, and YouTube (Dev, Buschman, and Bowen 2010). According to Muñiz and Schau (2011), conversations are related to brands and products within brand sites. There have been various names given to all these different brand sites and this is all part of the creation and exchange of CGC (Chu and Kim 2011). These sites include special interest groups and blogs (e.g., review forums), community forums (e.g.,

Starbucks), collaborative websites (e.g., Wikipedia), microblogging sites (e.g., Twitter), social networking sites (e.g., Facebook), customer reviews (e.g., Yelp, Epinions, Amazon.com), and video mash-ups or better known as creativity works-sharing sites (e.g., YouTube). All these market-oriented conversations are nothing like the corporate-driven, calculated, and coordinated communications. All these types of CGC "disseminate multi-vocal marketing messages and meanings" (Berthon et al. 2007).

Since the introduction of the Internet, consumers have transformed from *passive bystanders* to *hunters* (Hanna, Rohm, and Crittenden 2011). *Passive bystanders* refers to consumers that are not in a dialogue with the advertisements that are created through traditional media. Whereas, *hunters* refer to consumers who are able to control the content and are in fact in a dialogue with the company's Internet-based marketing campaigns. Consumers now make their own content and propagate it on social media sites such as YouTube. As Campbell et al. (2011) asserted, "the creation of advertisings and brand-focused videos is no longer prerogative of the organization or its designated ad agency" (p. 87). When CGC is in the form of advertising, consumers create brand-focused messages with the intention to inform, persuade, and remind others (Berthon, Pitt, and Campbell 2008). CGC has the ability to influence consumers' perception toward a brand, destination, and company (Campbell et al. 2011; Lim, Chung, and Weaver 2012; Ye et al. 2011). Duan, Gu, and Whinston (2008) demonstrated in their study that online consumer-generated reviews have a significant influence on sales of consumer products.

In the tourism context, Lim, Chung, and Weaver (2012) found that destination-marketing organizations have incorporated branding techniques with social media. Furthermore, consumers are gradually leaning toward the use of various social media for CGC to give them more information (Yoo and Gretzel 2011). Social media has become a powerful communication tool for consumers to share their experience, which in turn influences their decision-making process. CGC does not comprise just written reviews; it can also be in media and advertising forms. Litvin, Goldsmith, and Pan (2008) added that consumer-generated media websites have grown to be one of the prominent platforms in improving information accessibility and for enhancing consumers' decision-making processes. Ayeh (2015) pointed out that there is a growing interest in consumer-generated media and social media in general, but not all consumers are convinced about the use of consumer-generated media in their decision-making process (Burgess et al. 2011). This is probably because CGC "poses a challenge when it is in the form of advertising" (Campbell et al. 2011, p. 87).

Consumers' Role as Co-Creators in CGC

The idea of consumers as co-producers or co-creators is not novel in the marketing field. Theoretical models have been developed in this idea within the B2C relationship research area—one of which is the widely applied service-dominant logic (S-D logic). Vargo and Lusch (2004) argued that from the traditional, goods-based, manufacturing perspective, "the producer and consumer are usually viewed as ideally separated in order to enable maximum manufacturing efficiency" (p. 11). Based on their S-D logic model, they argue that from a service-centered perspective, the consumer is always involved in the production of value. However, they noted that for these services to be delivered, customers are still required to have the knowledge to use and adapt. Essentially, the development of this model indicates that the role of consumers is not just "target"; rather they are an operant resource (co-producer) in the entire value and service chain. Yi and Gong (2013) developed a customer value co-creation behavior scale to measure two elements of customers' co-creation behavior. These two elements are: customer participation behavior and customer citizenship. The former measures consumers' information-seeking, information-sharing, responsible behavior and personal interaction, whereas the latter focuses on feedback, advocacy, helping, and tolerance (p. 1279).

S-D logic, although heavily applied in the service context, is often used by marketing practitioners toward engaging their consumers with their product and service development. One way in which these consumers are involved in value creation is through their contribution of information on blogs, websites, review site, and on any social media platforms such as Facebook. For example, Doritos is one company that encourages their existing customers to co-create new products.

Humphreys and Grayson (2008) argued that co-creation for use and co-creation for value exchange (for others) should be distinguished. The difference between these two processes lies in their orientation. Co-creation for use is performed by a specific consumer for his or her own benefit, whereas co-creation for others is to benefit other consumers. Witell et al. (2011) claim that the aim of co-creation for use is to enjoy the production process and its outcome, whereas co-creation for others is to provide an idea, share knowledge, or participate in the development of a product or service that can be of value for other consumers.

Witell et al. (2011) argued that consumers play an important role in the production process. Furthermore, they posit that an organization must learn to develop its collaborative competence to move away from the perception that consumers are a source of information, and toward treating the consumer as an "active contributor with knowledge and skills" (p. 9). Companies not only need to engage consumers in the collaborative, participative, and contributive process; they also need these consumers to distribute the content forward. Hence, the term social curation (Villi, Moisander, and Joy 2012). Social curation is the next generation of collaborative effort where consumers become part of a company's marketing strategy.

CHAPTER 2

Consumer-Generated Content and Web 2.0

The media space has now changed its focus from product-centric to consumer-centric media exposure. The nature of the Internet has greatly added value to content and file sharing applications in the virtual space. This has positively shaped the creation and distribution mechanisms for consumer-generated content (CGC). With the focus now on consumers, the virtual space is highly personalized and consumers can tailor their media exposure to their specific needs and desires (Liang, Lai, and Ku 2006).

Why is tailored exposure important in the marketing world? When a user can tailor his or her exposure on the Internet, the release of information is according to the user's provision. Further, through Web-based applications that collect information through CGC platforms (e.g., social networking sites [SNS]), information will circle around consumers rather than the publisher. This implies that privacy and security issues are at stake, therefore highlighting the importance of tailored exposure. Again, this is a move from publisher-centric to consumer-centric. As CGC activities continue to evolve and dominate the consumer market in terms of communication medium, there will be more and more applications that will be used with the Web 2.0 application.

Really Simple Syndication, also known as RSS, is a technology that enables a consumer to use and access information in a more manageable space that is both customized and relevant (www.usa.gov). Web 2.0 and other collective software is built on RSS as it gives consumers the flexibility and accessibly to create or simply use the information on the Internet, or both. With the explosion of online information, which eventually led to the creation of CGC, company-based message producers are slowly losing their power to CGC. This power shift in the industry has called for greater control of the social media as well as for gaining a deeper understanding of consumers' motivation to create and consume media content. The greater the reliance on CGC, the greater the variety of choices available for consumers (Severin and Tankard 1992).

The relationship between Web 2.0 and CGC will likely increase the way people search for information, read, gather, and develop consumer information (Ye et al. 2011). This relationship between Web 2.0 and CGC provides a tremendous opportunity for e-commerce (Sigala 2008). Ye et al. (2011) posit that in e-commerce, CGC may serve as a new form of word-of-mouth (WOM) for products or services or their providers (p. 635).

Web 2.0 allows open communication with an emphasis on Web-based communities of users. Such an open communication enables more outlets for sharing different types of information. As users (consumers) utilize the Web 2.0 function, new platforms such as blogs and Wikis are born, which are considered components of Web 2.0. Often consumers see Web 2.0 as an online leisure activity platform more than a go-to information hub.

Categories of CGC

CGC houses several different platforms that are often referred to as social media. The use of social media on the Internet has changed the way information is searched and contributed (Williams et al. 2012). Although the term social media has multiple definitions, Blackshaw (2008) considers it an Internet-based application, also known as Web 2.0. This application is relevant to consumers' activities such as "posting," "tagging," or "blogging." Blackshaw and Nazzaro (2006, p. 4) claimed that CGC is "a mixture of fact and opinion, impression and sentiment, founded and unfounded tidbits, experiences, and even rumor." CGC is produced, shared, and used by consumers who have the desire to share their knowledge with each other on products, brands, services, and issues (Blackshaw and Nazzaro 2006).

Kaplan and Haenlein (2010) categorized social media into six different categories for CGC: collaborative projects (e.g., Wikipedia), blogs and microblogs (e.g., Twitter), content communities (e.g., YouTube), SNSs (e.g., Facebook), virtual world games (e.g., World of War Craft), and virtual worlds (e.g., Second Life). Regardless of the classification of each social interactive platform, each social media type has its strengths and designated purpose. Qualman (2011) stated that 93 percent of businesses use social networking for their marketing and branding activities. This is an indication of how many potential clients are attracted toward online surfing and how a SNS like Facebook increases a company's equity and its brand value.

As a part of an organization's promotional effort through more diverse communication outlets, many organizations have taken advantage of social media for their CGC, turning it into a new hybrid component of their integrated marketing communications (IMC) effort. By using social media, organizations are able to establish strong and lasting relationships with their consumers (Mangold and Faulds 2009; Weinberg and Pehlivan 2011). Social media has a unique ideology and technology as it allows consumers to generate and exchange content on the foundations of Web 2.0 (Kaplan and Haenlein 2011). There are a variety of social media out-lets built on an information-sharing format. These SNSs include Face-book, Pinterest, YouTube, and Flickr (creativity works-sharing sites), Wikipedia (collaborative sites), and also Twitter, a microblogging site. Among these various social media sites, SNSs have been the most popular format among researchers, practitioners, educators, and policy makers (Ellison and Boyd 2013; Roblyer et al. 2010).

Further, many consumers have started using social media in place of e-mail. Since 2006, the instant messaging options have already outpaced e-mail as an online activity (Pew Research Center 2007). The nature of social media encourages high levels of self-disclosure as well as a wider social presence. These social media forms have enabled consumers to connect with each other easily and quickly. Consumers who are participants of social media share opinions and thoughts on the products and services they purchased or consumed as well as exchange information on a par-ticular topic. Owing to the nature of social media, platforms like Face-book have become the consumer's destination for consumer-to-consumer (C2C) conversations, as well as the CGC widely known as WOM. Fur-ther, several researchers (Kim and Gupta 2012; Sweeney, Soutar, and

Mazaarol 2008) recognize the importance and influence of WOM on consumers' decision-making process.

Characteristics of CGC Consumers

In this section, we will look at the different characteristics that shape the behavior of each CGC consumer through social media. Several companies use social media to host their CGC. Therefore, it is important to look at social media users as they usually consume, participate, or contribute content via social media platforms. According to Forrester Research (blogs. forrester.com), social media users are classified by what is known as Social Technographics® Scores. Since 2007, Forrester's Social Technographics Ladder has been one of the widely used tools in determining the different types of social media users. However, as technology advances and people become more adaptable toward social media usage, marketers are no longer in the position of understanding whether their customers use social media. Rather, they are challenged with understanding how effective social media is in interacting with their customers.

Since the maturity of the social media consumer market, Forrester developed a new framework that helps marketers' analyze people's social behavior and benefits from this social media evolution. This model is known as the Social Technographics® Scores (Figure 2.1).

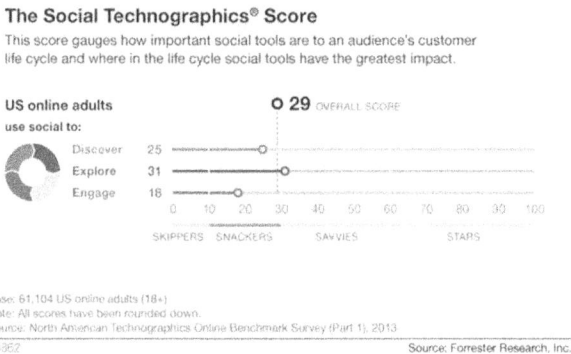

The Social Technographics® Score

This score gauges how important social tools are to an audience's customer life cycle and where in the life cycle social tools have the greatest impact.

US online adults use social to:		O **29** OVERALL SCORE
Discover	25	
Explore	31	
Engage	18	

0   10   20   30   40   50   60   70   80   90   100

SKIPPERS   SNACKERS   SAVVIES   STARS

Base: 61,104 US online adults (18+)
Note: All scores have been rounded down.
Source: North American Technographics Online Benchmark Survey (Part 1), 2013
73362   Source: Forrester Research, Inc.

Figure 2.1 U.S. Social Technographics Score

According to Forrester Research, this scoring system helps marketers to develop a successful social strategy in two stages:

1. Overall score, and
2. The discover, explore, and engage factors.

The overall score refers to how active consumers are in using social tools as well as how important these social tools are within their customer lifecycle and how willing they are in engaging brands on social media.

Like the Social Technographics Ladder, there are also audience categories. These categories range from high engagement with brands on social media to low engagement with brands on social media. Next, we look at these categories:

Social Stars—audiences who score high in their engagement with brands on social media will fit into this category. When a company has such a category in its customer base, it is an indication that it is time to make social media a centerpiece of the company's marketing effort.

Social Savvies or Social Snackers—audiences who fall into this middle range category comprise individuals who use social media moderately. In other words, if a company finds that the majority of its audience falls in this category, it should start thinking of using social media as a supporting tool in their marketing plan.

Social Skippers—audiences who belong to this category are known to be inactive social media users. In other words, companies that have the majority of their customers in this category should start shifting some of their resources from social media to other channels. This is largely due to the communication channel preferences of these customers. Moving certain resources (e.g., financial resources) into traditional media such as TV may prove to be influential for a successful marketing plan.

The second stage highlights the factors that inform companies where social tools are important in a marketing plan. Once companies have a better understanding of their social tool usage (heavy to light) in their marketing plan, they will need to know the types of social interactions being sought by their target consumers. Ranging from high to low, if a company's customer base is generally comprised of high *discover factor* individuals, it is likely that the company will have its customers' permission to use social reach strategies such as WOM.

However, if the *explore factor* is the highest, it indicates that the targeted consumers have a high preference for social interactions. Thus, investing in social depth strategies such as the development of a virtual community and implementations of reviews to the website is highly preferred.

The last factor in the second stage is the *engage factor*. If the company's consumer base is mainly filled with consumers with a high engage factor, then SNSs such as Facebook should be favored in its social relationship strategy. In other words, companies need not invest in white label social media platforms.

CGC—eWOM

The purpose of WOM is to allow consumers to exchange information with each other. It is essential in influencing their attitudes toward a particular product or service (Katz and Lazarsfeld 1995; Solomon 2014). WOM is believed to be a very powerful marketing communications tool as it creates a higher level of trust compared to company-generated persuasive messages. Companies are often biased in the messages they deliver, solely because they want to generate more sales. Thus, consumers often rely on CGC (i.e., WOM) when they search for information that forms the basis of their purchasing intent. WOM is no longer a face-to-face occurrence. It has expanded into the virtual world, creating a whole new platform for informal sources. Electronic WOM, henceforth referred to as eWOM, is facilitated by Internet-based media.

eWOM is defined as a statement that represents either a positive or negative statement made by potential, actual, or former customers on a product, service, or company. These statements are readily available to a large group of people via the Internet (Hennig-Thurau et al. 2004). eWOM occurs on a wide variety of virtual communication channels, including SNSs, blogs, e-mails, C2C review sites, discussion board or community forums, and instant messaging (Dwyer 2007; Hung and Li 2007). As eWOM spreads in the virtual world through these channels, marketers can take advantage of such a platform to gain a better understanding of consumers' decision-making processes, attitudes toward a product, brand, or service as well as the company's website. In fact, many companies create their own page, for example, on Facebook, to have a closer connection with their customers to meet the shift from company to customer demand. This is also known as relationship marketing.

The Case of L'Oréal and Estee Lauder

According to Shen and Bissell (2013), social media has been used, particularly Facebook, to "increase brand awareness and reinforce brand loyalty" (p. 646). They argue that the use of social media has changed consumers' decision-making process which has led companies to shift their focus from being product-centric to consumer-centric, and from information delivery to an exchange of information (p. 647).

Content creation is no longer a one-sided effort (e.g., company), rather it is combined with eWOM approaches, which are consumer-contributed (i.e., CGC). Although Shen and Bissell's (2013) study was situated in the beauty industry, it revealed a paucity for theoretical and empirical investigation in several other industries. Sengupta (2012) claims that an SNS, such as Facebook, has become one of the fastest growing ways for companies and businesses to promote their brands and products and to turn a one-way communication into an interactive model of communication. Social media networking sites such as Facebook have created "a mature WOM viral scenario for product promotion and brand management" (Shen and Bissell 2013, p. 647).

Often, companies and business use social media to promote their information. However, "it is not the only way to make profits" (Shen and Bissell 2013, p. 648). Rather, the collection of thoughts and advice from consumers via other activities such as Q&A or calendar sharing may be perceived as a more beneficial way to achieve brand loyalty.

Evidently, consumers' willingness to contribute toward posts, such as a "like" or "comment," on social media shows the strength and uniqueness for brands. Shen and Bissell (2013) added, eWOM is not a one-sided communication, either from the company or from the consumers. It needs to be interactive and engaging. In addition, Galloway (2012) found that "numb responses times … led to a decline in engage rates of almost 50 percent" in just one year (p. 2). In other words, timely responses by companies toward consumers are vital in keeping the eWOM interaction active. As this eWOM content accumulates, companies will take advantage of its presence to build traffic to its website as an interactive form of communication which leads to the creation of CGC.

CGC—Blogs

One category of CGC is a Weblog, also known as blog, which is a diary style website that generally offers observations and news that are posted in a chronological order. Within these blogs, there is space available for commentary, feedback from readers, and a column for recommended links. Bloggers are scrutinized in the messages they post on the blogging universe, also known as the blogsphere. Although certain studies examine the credibility of online media, scholars have not paid attention to the credibility of the users that judge the quality of Weblogs (Johnson and Kaye 2004). Although Weblogs have received criticism, their popularity is undeniable. According to Johnson and Kaye (2004), the number of blog users increased from an estimated 30,000 in 1998 to at least 3 million by the beginning of 2004. Another reason for the blog's increased popularity is the content it generates. Many blog users are interested in politics and therefore are easily persuaded by tech-savvy politicians. This niche market of blog users may be small but their influence may have exceeded the expected readership. Despite the initial aggression by many journalists, they have gradually seen the blog as a trustworthy source of information and do not hesitate to rely on them for relevant information and inspiration for ideas. One of the main reasons for the blogs' dependability is its capability in bringing stories to light when traditional media refuses to. Cho and Huh (2010) argued that even though the use of blogs by corporations is still small, the number is increasing. Blogs by corporations (hereafter corporate blogs) have a twofold purpose: internal and external. Companies use internal blogs as a communication tool to enhance internal communications among their staff as well as external stakeholders.

On the other hand, corporations also offer consumers an opportunity to contribute toward their corporate blogs by reviewing products, services, and technologies offered by the companies of which they are customers. Some of these consumer bloggers are compensated, whereas others are voluntary (Ghazisaeedi, Steyn, and Van Heerden 2012). Droge, Stanko, and Pollitte (2010) posit that blogs have been an important communication tool as they allow information distribution through the Internet as well as have knowledge-sharing capability. Communication and marketing companies use blogs as a market research tool to analyze the current market place and as an evaluation tool for their business' welfare (Xifra and Huertas 2008). Further, blogs allow consumers to cocreate value with companies by sharing their experiences about their purchased products with the company (Droge, Stanko, and Pollitte 2010). On the contrary, since blogs are generally contributed by consumers (Mutum and Wang 2010), blogs have enabled consumers to take control of the products' popularity by allowing them to contribute with instant feedback and using the blog as a strong eWOM (Droge, Stanko, and Pollitte 2010).

Consumer-Generated Websites—Collaborative Sites

Wikipedia is a CGC platform on which consumers can contribute content that are of interest to them. For someone who is new to online contribution, it may seem a little overwhelming with the amount of content that is posted on the site. It is not true that a contributor needs to know everything and anything about posting content on Wikipedia. It is important to know how to use our common sense when we write and edit content. Wikipedia allows contributors to create, revise, and edit articles. These features encourage contributors to contribute content to its best accuracy.

Many college professors use Wikipedia as a part of their lesson plan; for example students are required to create their very own encyclopedia as part of their assignment. Although there are protocols in using Wikipedia, one cannot break the platform. The good thing about Wikipedia is that it is a work-in-progress project. Very often, students are asked to work collaboratively on their classmate's work to edit any incomplete or poorly written pieces. As we practice and as time permits, a poorly expressed article will become an excellent piece of article.

Wikipedia has also been a popular collaborative hub for several companies including Pixar and Red Ant. Red Ant, a web design company based in Sydney, Australia, uses Wikipedia as the main collaboration hub between its employees and its clients. Red Ant explains that this hub is used to share and gain approval from its client for a particular design. In addition to back and forth iterations among developers, the client also gets involved by e-mailing the link of a diagram or adds comments on the page (stewartmedar.com). There may be opportunities for product marketing on Wikipedia, especially for larger companies. However, generally product marketers are unlikely to benefit from what they would find on a Wikipedia page (King 2011).

The Core of CGC

The popularity of CGC among consumers is soaring (DeMers 2014). The reason for such popularity is partly due to the ease of usage and perceived usefulness of CGC (Ayeh, Au, and Law 2013). With the principles of human–computer interaction, the software design for a majority of these CGC platform supports users' activities. Furthermore, Preece (2000) and others (Flavián, Guinalíu, and Gurrea 2006; Preece, Nonnecke, and Andrews 2004) argued that if the software has great usability, and is consistent, controllable, and predictable, users will be able to use the platform with ease, with efficiency, and have a pleasant experience. There are two features that predominately attract users to participate in CGC: ease of use and perceived usefulness. These two features are arguably strong determinants in enhancing consumers' need for satisfaction.

Ease of Use

An important feature when attracting users to a CGC platform is the ease of usage. Ultimately, if a product or service is easy for a consumer to use, be involved with, or produce, it will be key to attracting more people. On the other hand, if a product or service has several complicated steps to maneuver, then users will just get frustrated and eventually give up the idea of using the platform. This brings us to the topic of why consumers are so attracted to Wikipedia. For science-based knowledge, users often flock to Wikipedia due to its convenience. Although Wikipedia has a drawback in that its accuracy is questionable when compared with other sources, people rank convenience over accuracy (Head and Eisenberg 2010; Rainie and Tancer 2007). Companies that benefited from using Wikipedia include IBM, Sony Ericsson, and Red Ant (www.stewartmader.com).

Another example is the use of YouTube. Regardless of whether a person is uploading or watching a video for a particular purpose, the outcome from this source is phenomenal. People often weigh the gains and losses for any decision they make (see Prospect Theory). Thus, if a user is able to find out more information and gain more knowledge from an easily accessible source, then that source will highly likely attract people to consume, participate, and produce. Essentially, the meaning of easy usage means to put in little effort (e.g., few clicks for uploading a video) for a greater output (e.g., abundance of information).

In theory, Bentham's utility theory (Read 2007) has been used to explain this "ease of use" phenomenon. This theory is an evaluative framework for alternative choices made by individuals or groups, or institutions. The definition of utility refers to the level of satisfaction that each choice provides for the decision maker. Essentially, this theory assumes that any decision is made based on which choice has the highest utility (i.e., satisfaction) for the decision maker. This rationale is based on the utility maximization principle. Fishburn (1968) explained that when utility theory is used on a practical perspective, people's choices and decisions are the main concerns. This theory also explains "people's preferences, judgments of preference, worth value, and goodness or any of a number of similar concept" (p. 335).

We are currently in a digitally reliant society where there is a wealth of information available at our fingertip; wealth of information creates a poverty of attention and there is a need to allocate the attention efficiently through the abundance of information in order to consume it. Thus, with a simple design and accessibility, it will maximize people's satisfaction at the same time allowing a degree of control. CGC has been serving its importance by not only helping people with attention allocation but also providing great gratification.

CGC platforms have become a virtual gathering place for different types of audiences and have inevitably changed traditional media perception. With the presence of social media, CGC has become more and more appealing to large groups of individuals because of its usability and level of gratification obtained from consuming, participating, and producing CGC. CGC is not only a source of entertainment for people, but it can also serve as a source of education. CGC is multifaceted as it offers a wide variety of resources for people with different needs. With the nature of CGC, individuals have changed their way of online searching and the concept of trust with online information. Despite the multiple uses of CGC, these sites are often utilized the most for entertainment purposes. For example, YouTube has changed the perception of entertainment. It is no longer the traditional movie night or Saturday Night Live shows; rather entertainment has become a light and digestible snack that users can consume at a fast speed and at a high frequency. In addition, in regards to mood management, people may seek to use CGC to comfort them, leading them to a whole different world, or it could create an emotional stir. This alteration of mood states is still a prevailing argument.

Despite the positive attributes of CGC, several questions still remain: Is the ultimate goal of CGC to build up a community or to enhance one's self-concept (e.g., self-expression)? With users sitting in front of a screen, is it really an engagement with society? If they were to go offline, can these individuals be engaged at the same level? If they can't, wouldn't that be a contradiction of the core purpose of CGC?

Perceived Usefulness

Online consumer reviews contain open-ended viewpoints and ratings from consumers (Park and Kim 2009). Open-ended viewpoints are textual assessments of the positives and negatives of the quality of a product or service. Ratings, on the other hand, is a summary of numeric statistics. According to Cheung, Lee, and Rabjohn (2008), the perceived usefulness of a review has been found to be a significant predictor of consumer's intent to comply with a review. Mudambi and Schuff (2010) defined perceived usefulness as "a measure of perceived values in the purchase decision-making process" (p. 186). Ratings that are on the extreme end of the evaluation scale (i.e., 1–5 star ratings) are perceived to be more useful than neutral ratings (Danescu-Niculescu-Mizil et al. 2009). Sen and Lerman (2007), on the other hand, found that the usefulness of reviews is also reliant on the popularity of product ratings (e.g., negative reviews are more impactful than positive reviews).

Danescu-Niculescu-Mizil et al. (2009) argued that the usefulness of reviews goes above and beyond the star or numerical ratings or both. Willemsen et al. (2011) added that the important drivers of a review's perceived usefulness can be based on three content characteristics within the open-ended reviews—that is, "expertise claims, review valence and argumentation" (p. 21). They also found four characteristics that have a significant effect on consumers' perceived usefulness of online consumer reviews. Purchase price, one of the four characteristics, had a significant negative effect on perceived usefulness of online consumer reviews. The remaining three characteristics—review length, star rating, and location disclosure (i.e., residential location of the reviewer)—had a significant positive effect on perceived usefulness of online consumer reviews. Willemsen et al. (2011) concluded that longer reviews that have more star ratings and contain information on the reviewer's place of residence are considered more useful—"as are reviews of relatively low-priced products" (p. 29).

In addition, Pollach (2008) discovered that when reviewers claim to have expert knowledge on a particular product, their evaluation of the product under consideration is likely to be perceived as useful. Furthermore, Hu and Sundar (2010) explained that the authority heuristic often steers people's judgment of a review. Review valence was also found to have a marginally positive main effect on perceived usefulness (Willemsen et al. 2011). Review valence is determined on the basis of whether the review offers a positive or negative comment. Willemsen et al. (2011) argued that "the more positive (negative) the valence of a review, the more (less) likely people are to purchase the reviewed product" (p. 22). In addition, they also found out that review valence is not consistent across all product types. Their results showed an interaction effect—demonstrating that the negative effect was prevalent for *experience* products. Referring back to classic literature, Aike and West (1991) used a slope analysis to demonstrate that the perceived usefulness of consumer review valence had a negative effect when the product discussed falls under the *experience* product category. Whereas, a positive effect is prevalent when the product discussed falls in the *search* product category.

Schindler and Bickart (2005) claim that argument density is a significant predictor of consumers' perceived usefulness of online reviews. Their results show that online reviews are regarded as more useful when the product evaluation is accompanied by a high number of arguments. Similarly, their results also show that argument diversity was also a significant indicator of perceived usefulness of online consumer reviews. Argument diversity for online reviews means that reviews for a product should be spread between positive and negative in order for consumers to perceive its usefulness in their decision-making process.

Furthermore, negative information does not impact all products; rather, their results show that review valence is dependent on the type of products being evaluated (e.g., *experience* vs. *search* products) (Willemsen et al. 2011). Contrary to previous research, negative eWOM showed a stronger impact on consumers' judgment and choices compared to objectively equivalent positive eWOM (Godes and Mayzlin 2004; Park, Lee, and Han 2007). Willemsen et al. (2011) found that negative eWOM was only effective on *experience* products and those reviews were perceived to be more useful than positive reviews. On the other hand, they discovered that when the product evaluated is classified as a *search* product, only positive reviews were perceived to be more useful. The results were explained using consumers' attributes such as familiarity and likings—they argue that positive eWOM becomes more prevalent in the situation where the product being evaluated is a *search* product because when such an evaluation is done, consumers tend to infuse their familiarity and likings with the product attributes before making the actual purchase. It is important for marketing practitioners to know which type of eWOM they should address depending on the type of products because of the differences in pre-purchase performance veracity (Park and Kim 2009; Xia and Bechwati 2008).

Based on Willemsen et al.'s (2011) results, consumers' perceived usefulness of online reviews includes the characteristics of the reviews on the surface level (e.g., star rating, reviewer identity disclosure). They extended on previous research (Chevalier and Mayzlin 2006; Ghose and

Ipeirotis 2009) and explained that these characteristics are regarded as heuristic cues, which can be processed with minimal effort. Furthermore, they used the Elaboration Likelihood Model (Petty and Cacioppo 1984) to argue that consumers use argument density and diversity to evaluate the usefulness of a review as these indicators are more central to the content of the review, which requires more elaborate processing (Petty and Cacioppo 1984). In addition, textual content of reviews is able to convey the subtle online interactions between consumers that is not attainable through star ratings (Resnick et al. 2000, p. 47).

Since argument diversity and density has an impact on consumers' perceived usefulness of online reviews, it suggests that web-masters of a website should consider a suitable format or layout for review spaces that encourages consumers to express both their positive and negative opinions and thoughts. By structuring the reviews in such a way, consumers will be able to fully utilize the comments during their decision-making process.

Consumer's Attitude Toward CGC

In relation to CGC, a consumer's attitude toward CGC derives from his or her perception of the value of the content, which then relates back to his or her beliefs and feelings. Studying the psychological aspect of a consumer's attitude with his or her relationship is no easy task. This is because of the various types of behavior that consumers would experience. Therefore, Fazio and Towles-Schwen (1999) categorize consumers' thought processes into spontaneous and deliberate. They explain that when consumers are experiencing spontaneous thought processes, the reaction and attitude formed will be passed on to their perceived image of the object in their immediate surroundings. They add that when a consumer experiences such a thought process, generally there are environmental cues that triggers a memory for the consumer, which indicates an imminent behavior. Any resulting behavior of a consumer is dependent on his or her attitude at a given time in a given situation. The consumer's behavior is also reliant on his or her past experiences with a similar situation (e.g., memory).

On the other hand, when consumers experience the deliberate processing approach, they do not place emphasis on pre-existing attitudes triggered by the environmental cues. Rather, they develop and build on raw data presented in the situation. Since this method of processing is considered deliberate, consumers form their attitudes based on their evaluation of the data. Essentially, what this means is that consumer will think about the potential consequences of engaging in a particular behavior when they consider the type of attitude they should form. It is reasonable to assume that the consumption of CGC is a deliberate behavior because it involves data-driven decisions. According to Fishbein and Ajzen's (1975) theory, attitude has a positive relationship with behavior. Thus, if there is a positive interaction regarding a piece of CGC, the consumer's attitude toward CGC consumption and creation should become more positive.

Between the two types of CGC thought processes, the deliberative processing route will lead to consumption behavior. However, if the CGC behavior is spontaneous then it will lead to creation behavior. Spontaneous type of behavior is often triggered by environmental cues, which suggests that an attitude and an action are required. Nonetheless, in order for consumers to embark on content creation, it will require both previous experience and the timeliness of the situation. Thus, if consumers have a positive attitude toward CGC in general, they will likely have a positive reaction toward creating their own CGC. This positive reaction will have an impact on how much consumers attempt to consume CGC and how much they are likely to create it.

Collaborative Behaviors: Consumption, Participation, and Production of CGC

The reason why consumers are intrigued with CGC concerns their internal motivations (Eastin and Daugherty 2005). CGC consumption is regarded as a deliberate and active behavior. This suggests that the internal motivation of such behavior happens because it is out to meet the needs of the consumers. This motivation forms an attitude, which ultimately influences behavior. Consumers' motivation varies, which means that depending on the level of motivation (high vs. low), consumers may choose one behavior over the other. For example, if the motivation for the consumer is to consume (i.e., look at) consumer-generated media and not to create, then it can also imply that the difference in the willingness to experience CGC is different. This is because there is a difference in the level of involvement (high versus low between the willingness to consume and the willingness to create content online).

The three suggested ways in which consumers are motivated to use CGC include: (1) consumption, (2) participation, and (3) production. *Consumption* is defined as usage of content (e.g., watch, read); it does not include participation. The second way, *participation*, acts as a two-way street. In other words, there is an interaction among the users and an interaction between the user (i.e., consumer) and content. This latter interaction includes activities such as posting of comments, sharing with others, and peer-to-peer music sharing. *Production*, on the other hand, is the creation and publication of one's personal content such as photos and videos. In other words, it implies self-produced content that is contributed online. In essence, when consumers choose to consume, they are browsing online for information and entertainment purposes.

These collaborative behaviors (consuming, participating, and producing), although separate, are actually interdependent of each other. These activities are representative of a gradual engagement with CGC. When an individual is exposed to a new activity, the level of involvement will be very minimal. In the context of SNSs, consumers begin their involvement as consumers or lurkers. In order to proceed to the next step of involvement, people visit the CGC sites to consume content, absorbing information but not comfortable to participate.

After a period of familiarization, consumers will eventually come out of their shell and begin to participate through interaction. Apart from a C2C interaction, information consultation is also a type of interaction. With such an interaction in place, consumers will gradually establish their position, building and maintaining social relationships with people in the virtual world. In the last phase, which is when consumers are very comfortable with the social media platform as well as self-identification, they will start to product content. This behavior is also regarded as the highest level of involvement in a CGC activity.

When consumers start to produce content and share it in their online communities, it is an indication of the their self-expression and self-actualization (Heinonen 2011; Shao 2008). It is important to note that not every consumer will follow the consecutive phases of establishing their identity online. Though, it is a natural path for any newcomer to follow, some people may have a higher level of confidence in producing their own original content. For example, a consumer may not feel the need to respond to a fellow consumer online, but is comfortable with producing and publishing his or her original work online. With the large amount of information published online, it may be assumed that there is a large number of consumer-producers. However, this assumption is false. Instead, the majority of consumers remain lurkers, and minority become contributors.

One of the main reasons for consumers to contribute their production online is to attract readers or lurkers. These contributors hope to solicit two-way responses: for example, comments and content dissemination to other CGC consumers. When there is a two-way interaction among CGC users, they are able to fulfill their social interaction needs, and even form friends within the virtual communities. The presence of responses for any content also encourages more creation from the original producers.

The activities of consumption, participation, and production comprise the lifecycle of consumers' CGC behavior. Since content production attracts the attention of several consumers, large amounts of information are available for people to consume and entertain themselves. Furthermore, participating is similar to consuming, in that it reinforces producers to produce more since there is a need for self-expression and self-actualization (Chen 2013). Nonetheless, it is important to note that the population of producers is just as important as the population of consumers. This is because without consumption or participation, there is no need or motivation to produce more content. Each consumer plays an important role in the CGC lifecycle. For example, participating consumers can interact with producers by posting comments, rating, and sharing with others. All these behaviors not only enhance consumers' online experiences in the form of entertainment, but they also enhance knowledge (Gummerus et al. 2012).

Sometimes, comments from fellow consumers are easier to comprehend compared to information provided by the company's sales representative or information posted on its website. Why? This is because these former or current consumers relate their experiences using their own words without resorting to jargon. For example, on YouTube, there is an option for the creator (person who uploads the video) to enable public comments. Consumers who view the comments could then freely write what they thought of the video or they could simply just use the comments to gain a better understanding of that content. Review sites such as Yelp have ratings as well as reviews as the core features of their service. These ratings, rankings, and reviews allow consumers to find the best deal in town or the most popular store. As for the "sharing with" function on social media, consumers may wish to share the knowledge or share the content with someone whom they think would appreciate this information or who shares the same interests.

Consumers' Motivation in Consuming CGC

Studies have shown that there are motives to why people use social media (e.g., Bronner and de Hoog 2010a, 2010b; Yoo and Gretzel 2008, 2012). According to Graber (1993) and others (McQuail 2000), there two typical motives to why people use social media: (1) information seeking and (2) entertainment. Equipped with this knowledge of the motivation behind social media users, marketers are able to better target their intended audiences.

Information Seeking

People seek information online to raise their level of awareness on certain topics, knowledge about themselves, others, and even society. With this thirst for knowledge, CGC has been gaining considerable attention, for example, a CGC platform like Wikipedia. Although it is not academically "approved" for use due to its reliability issue, people frequently visit the site to obtain general information about subjects that are of interest to them. The reason behind the choice of Wikipedia is because information is readily available in a concise manner.

Few of the main reasons that several universities discourage the use of Wikipedia are its questionable integrity and the source of information. Anyone can create new topics or edit items as they wish. All information that is created is immediately available to the world. Referring back to the theory of self-expression, people who contribute to such CGC sites may develop a sense of self-importance. They believe that their contribution has an impact on society and their action supports their self-image as an efficacious individual (Bandura 2001).

Entertainment

The other purpose for use of social media is entertainment. Bowman and Willis (2003) argued that consumers who use the social network site such as Facebook, are learning "how to make sense of things from their peers on just about any subject" (p. 40). With the increase in the number of search engines available, CGC has been a main source of influence in how information should be "searched." Blackshaw and Nazzaro (2006) noticed that when a consumer searches for something on search engines like Google, it is highly likely that a CGC site will surface first before any company's website. Furthermore, consumers tend to trust fellow consumers more than professional advertisers or marketers. As compared to information seeking, marketers consider consumers who use social media for entertainment purposes as a more important target market (Rafaeli and Sudweeks 1997).

Despite the difference in definition between entertainment and mass media, Ruggiero (2000) and others (Lee and Ma 2012) posit that majority of the people tend to lump those two categories together. Although it may be incorrect to assume that entertainment and mass media are synonymous, the birth of YouTube triggers such confusion as it is one of the main mass media platforms used by people globally for entertainment purposes. Consumers visit the YouTube website and watch entertainment-related channels such as sports, music, comedy, and drama. Miller (2007) labeled social media platforms such as YouTube as a "snack food." This synonym mirrors the digestible attribute of a typical snack: small, light, and compact. These so-called snacks are catered toward individuals who have time constraints. Miller (2007) argued that pop culture is consumed in "bite-sized" pieces just like cookies or chips. In other words, these snacks are consumed in minutes but over an increased frequency and at maximum speed.

Indeed, many of the YouTube videos are just a few minutes long. The reason for such a bite-size technique is to (1) entertain oneself without being tied to the screen for a long period of time, and (2) retain concentration span. YouTube is a very innovative entertainment idea as it is able to meet people's need for high-speed entertainment without compromising on the quality and quantity of videos. It may be a desire for some to escape from reality and indulge in a carefree, relaxing, and enjoyable moment or even for emotional release (Katz, Blumer, and Gurevitch 1974). Thus, using CGC entertainment like YouTube is more favorable over traditional media such as television and magazines. Another benefit of using CGC entertainment is its power of altering prevailing mood states of consumers. Marketing companies thus take advantage of this ability of CGC entertainment to captivate their consumers in conveying messages on their product or service. With a positively regulated mood (e.g., happy), the acceptance level of digesting the advertised message will be higher than the message portrayed from traditional media.

Consumers' Motivation in Participating in CGC

When a consumer chooses to participate, he or she will be engaged in social interaction and community development. There has been an enormous leap in the number of users active on SNSs. According to a Nielsen Social Media report (2012), in an average month, Americans spend approximately 7 hours on Facebook alone. If a consumer chooses to produce his own content, he then ultimately had the desire to express his inner self or what Maslow considers self-actualization. According to Johnson and Knobloch-Westerwick (2014), individuals "may select social media sites content with the motivation to regulate mood" (p. 33). Prior research determined that the maintenance and development of social capital fosters social media use (Ellison, Steinfield, and Lampe 2011), as well as aiding in reducing an individual's loneliness and boredom (Lampe, Ellison, and Steinfield 2008). Furthermore, it has been researched that when an individual views his or her own profile, it boosted his or her self-esteem (Gentile et al. 2012). All these results are tied to a psychological theory known as mood management theory (Bryant and Davies 2006). Apart from boosting one's self-esteem, individuals who are stressed can also view YouTube clips and find some relaxation. Bored individuals can search for excitatory materials, and through this method, they can bring their physiological arousal and affect back to optimal, comfortable levels. Consumers' choice on YouTube is largely inclined to videos that are "most viewed" or "most rated." This also suggests that YouTube has a broader range of stimuli choices when compared to traditional media such as television channels.

Participating for Social Interaction and Community Development

As discussed earlier, users play the role of consumers (see role theory) when using the media as a source of information. Apart from consumption for information retrieval purposes, consumers also participate by engaging and interacting with the content as well as with users on consumer-generated sites. So how do consumers interact with the content and other users or consumers on the same social media? Consumers interact with content when they (1) rate the content, (2) click on the "star" to save the sites onto their favorites list, (3) click on the "share" button to share the information with people they know, (4) post comments, and (5) post the content to their SNSs (e.g., Facebook wall). These are some of the examples of what is meant by consumer interaction. A C2C interaction on the other hand, as understood by the name, is interaction with other fellow users on the same SNS. The methods of communication include the following: e-mails, instant messaging, chatrooms, community boards, and walls. The consumer-content interaction may be considered as an indirect communication, whereas a C2C interaction may be considered a form of direct communication. Regardless of the contact (direct or indirect), these forms of communication are able to fulfill the consumers' need for interaction (Chan and Li 2010).

As McKenna and Bargh (1999) argue, since the inception of the Internet, social media has become a place for social interaction. Back in the early 2000s, Internet websites such as Yahoo and Excite among many others, that provided electronic venues for people to communicate with people who don't necessary know each other. These venues include chat rooms, instant messaging, message boards, and e-mails. With the emergence and growing popularity of different social media platforms, engaging in social media activities has become an integral of people's lives worldwide. Regardless of whether it is a simple search on movie reviews, or obtaining advice for a major life decision, there are several different social sites available for different users for different purposes. Despite the growing popularity and strong presence of the social media, there is still a debate on whether the Internet can fulfill people's interaction social needs.

Some scholars have viewed the Internet as an inherently antithetical contribution toward the nature of our lives. On the contrary, the Internet was perceived as a solution to reduce loneliness, decreased depression, hostility, and isolation. The Internet was also believed to be a tool that helps in enhancing one's self-esteem in the society, encourage greater likeability among others (e.g. peers), as well as to promote a conducive environment for others to feel accepted by others in the society. It is also a tool to widen social circles (McKenna and Bargh 1999). How do we know that the Internet has wide acceptance and greater favorability over other types of media? By observing the success of CGC platforms such as Facebook, Twitter, LinkedIn, Pinterest, and many other SNSs, it is evident that SNSs have a positive perspective among Internet users. In the United States, more than 74 percent of online users are engaged on online social sites (www.pewinternet.org). Back in the early 2000s, social sites were primarily used to reinforce preexisting friendships or used to make new friends, or for both. Despite SNSs being criticized for causing individuals to be antisocial in face-to-face interactions, they have their own advantages. A few advantages suggested by Van Dijk (2006) was that since there is no distraction such as nonverbal communication, consumers are able to concentrate more on the content by reading, watching, or listening intently to the content. In addition, it also allows consumers to loosen up and maintain an informal conversation. Therefore, SNS has become one of the most acceptable CGC platforms where brands can engage with their target audience and vice versa (Ruchko 2014).

Virtual Communities

Online interaction is not just a come and go session where people keep their conversation short. It is also an opportunity where people's participation contributes toward the development and maintenance of communities. For example, Starbucks has an established virtual community on Facebook. These virtual communities are formed when people of the same interests and concerns gather to carry out public discussions. These discussions are long to an extent where strangers become community members where they form a relationship with one another (Rheingold 2000). These virtual communities are places where individuals who share similar interests are able to voice their opinions and concerns in a nondiscriminatory environment. Furthermore, as explained by Tajfel's (1982) Social Identity Theory (SIT), people feel a sense of belonging when they are associated with a group. Similar to a face-to-face group, virtual communities also allow members to feel that their feelings are being shared and their needs are met through their commitment with each other (McMillan and Chavis 1986).

Virtual communities can be created solely on a community site or they may be created on any SNS as a subgroup (e.g., Facebook). These communities represent an identity where people connect and interact regarding shared interests and support. In fact, these virtual communities can be perceived as important as physically located communities. Although scholars have determined that members have a set commitment that keeps the group going and the conversation alive, there is always the question of who initiates a conversation. According to Joyce and Kraut (2006), responding to C2C content is a useful first step in developing a virtual community. In fact, repeated actions could lead to positive reinforcement where consumers keep their posts constant. As long as there is a response on an initial post, the content provider will feel motivated to share more new materials. Thus, it is important for community members to be responsive to posts, regardless of the tone, to maintain meaningful content creation.

CGC is a platform that focuses on consumer-to-consumer or even company-to-consumer interactions. Individuals take advantage of the content and the presence of other human beings to create and develop an interaction. For example, LinkedIn has provided a large support for business professionals with business networking opportunities. Facebook, on the other hand, has provided support for social networking opportunities. Individuals fulfill their social needs through online interactions with others. When a relationship expands into a network, a virtual community is formed. People within this virtual community can share their interests, identity, and a sense of closeness. Since virtual communities are created around CGC, it is arguable that these virtual community members should respond to each other's comments or contribution as that is the core activity to strengthen dynamic content creation.

Consumers' Motivation in Producing CGC

For continuation of CGC, constant production is key. Without producing content, there will be no CGC available. Many ask the mind-boggling question as to how people are motivated to produce CGC. Before we discuss the motivations behind why consumers create content and post them on the Internet via various social media, we will first look at the overarching popularity of self-created entertainment. In the United States, majority of the self-published content is produced by youths. Consumers who belong to the Gen X group are also catching up on the trend and creating their own content on YouTube. The number of videos produced is on a considerable scale where individuals could actually earn a living from just creating YouTube videos. For example, there have been cases where consumers self-create videos on YouTube and become instant celebrities from sharing knowledge on how to put make-up. These individuals were scouted by make-up companies to promote the latter's products on the former's videos. Thus, CGC has grown exponentially and has become an outlet that is specifically designed for people to engage in a producing behavior.

Bowman and Willis (2003) explain that consumers may have the desire to produce content solely to inform and entertain other people. There are two underlying theories that attempt to explain the motivation behind CGC contributors. One is known as *self-expression*, and the other is *self-actualization*. *Self-expression* is defined as one's own expression on their identity. Essentially, individuals who are self-expressing are highlighting their individuality. McKenna and Bargh (1999) added that this concept assumes that people need to present their inner-self to the external environment. The rationale behind such behavior is because they want to exhibit their true selves. Now, how is this concept a motivator for consumer contribution to social media? By being actively engaged in blogging, video castings, and other self-highlighting activities, it allows individuals to showcase who they are by reflecting on their behavior online. Self-expression can either be explicit or implicit. Consumers who choose to use self-expression from an explicit approach would conduct their behavior through direct self-disclosure, whereas the implicit approach will be to focus more on the choice of words, style, and topic

(Shiu 2013; VanLear et al. 2005). Ultimately, consumers who contribute to social media willingly are individuals who have the desire to construct an image and to establish an identity for themselves (i.e., self-expression).

Criticism against consumers who try hard to self-express themselves to others are often from people who are trying to escape reality. Kokkoris and Kühnen (2015) argued that self-expression creates the sense of being excluded from humble beings, and other external factors such as sounds and emotions from our everyday existence. On the contrary, despite the cynicism behind why people want to self-express, this self-expression process can be seen as an attempt to control the impressions of how others see them (Bortree 2005; Dominick 1999). It is inevitable that we establish an image of a person even before we meet that individual in person. These images are created based on hearsay, gossip, and information that is not necessary true. Thus, as individuals, we engage in selective self-expression, even if the information transmitted through the communication process is rational. There will still be the selective impression that the sender has intended to engage in (Walther et al. 2009).

When individuals contribute toward social media, they often have an intention to exercise impression management. Their behavior is apparent in the context of the creation of personal home pages and blogs online. As all these activities are customized for each individual, who has a different objective of what type of impression he or she wants to make, he or she has the flexibility to stage an online performance through his or her personality. One way to ensure that the staged performance is circulated on the Internet is individuals to engage in marketing strategies where they present their "self," hopefully to attract readers and build supportive relationships with their fans or followers on their personalized sites (Dominick 1999). Individuals who use personal home pages to express themselves fall into two categories. For those who want to use webpages as a self-expressive tool, you will find more personal information compared to those who want to use their webpages as a professional tool. Some personalized home pages serve as personal blogs or vice versa. Regardless of the activity, those who see a need to self-express will use their blogs as a self-reflective account where they post their personal experiences (Hollenbaugh 2010; Trammell and Keshelashvili 2005). It was noted that

A-list bloggers are strong advocates of self-expression as they reveal more personal information than other bloggers.

Self-actualization motivates individuals to produce their own content on consumer-generated sites. *Self-actualization* is defined as the need to work on one's identity while reflecting back on one's personality (Harmon-Jones, Schmeichel, and Harmon-Jones 2009; Trepte 2005). Part of this self-actualization is to express oneself which is ultimately aimed at highlighting one's own identity. As discussed earlier, several CGC users engage in creating and producing content (e.g., blogging, video cast) to achieve self-expression. Self-expression is all about how one needs to highlight him or herself and to show who he or she is. In addition, self-expression also allows one to control how a third party perceives him or her to be. Furthermore, what motivates individuals to produce contents is their self-actualization and self-concept. The product that is produced is a reflection of their need to be recognized, become famous, or simply because of personal efficacy. All these CGC engagement reasons are interrelated. These activities help fulfill both an individual's social and psychological needs. It is important to note, however, that the path to consume, participate, and produce is a gradual process. Furthermore, not all individuals will go through all steps. Some may skip the second step and go directly to the third step. It all depends on the level of self-concept and confidence of each individual.

Self-actualization is the last need as designated by Maslow's hierarchy in his pyramid of needs. Unlike the motive for self-expression, self-actualization is primarily an unconscious behavior (Aarts and Dijksterhuis 2000; Berridge and Winkielman 2003). However, it can also be regarded as a psychological motive that drives one to attain a behavioral goal such as online production. For example, a social media contributor may want to seek recognition or personal efficacy (Bughin 2007). With accessibility, many social media users begin to dream about achieving instant fame. These regular social media users' use CGC platforms to publish their content with the primary motivation of fame. Take American make-up artist Michelle Phan as an example. She rose to fame through her blogs and has engaged in YouTube channels demonstrating make-up techniques since May 2007. With such exposure, Michelle has since gained recognition in the make-up industry and has been an endorser for some well-known make-up brands such as Lancôme and L'Oreal.

With large traffic on YouTube and other sites, many people are optimistic of becoming famous content producers someday. Thus, there will no doubt be an increase in the number of self-produced videos on CGC sites.

Consumers' and Companies' Perspectives on CGC

CGC can be presented in the form of "online testimonials, product reviews, and consumer-generated commercials" (Rodger, Thorson, and Jun 2014, p. 199). Such CGC is often referred to as customer evangelism (Muñiz and Schau 2011). These online reviews can either have a direct or indirect effect on consumers' decision to purchase a product or service (Ertimur and Gilly 2010). These activities are however not considered commercially motivated.

As consumers get more critical and skeptical about what products they purchase, the Internet becomes the source in their decision-making process. Regardless of the motivation behind Internet use, Internet users are encouraged to rate and review different kinds of services and products that they have had experience with. These types of reviews are known as consumer-generated eWOM. eWOM has been defined as "any positive or negative statement made by potential, actual or former customers about a product or company, which is made available to a multitude of people and institutions via the Internet" (Hennig-Thurau et al. 2004, p. 39). It is a type of online advertisement that takes advantage of the CGC platform.

Marketers have had the luxury of spreading commercialized information widely till the introduction of the Internet. From WOM to eWOM, the Internet has revolutionized how consumers obtain information and how quick and easy it is to obtain this information online. Spreading information online was once termed as "e-fluentials" (Sun et al. 2006) till 2004 when consumer-generated eWOM grabbed the spotlight (Hennig-Thurau et al. 2004). The main purpose for the birth of eWOM is to reduce the risk and the misleading information presented by private advertisements. eWOM is presumably contributed by a diverse array of "experts" who offer advice about what to buy and what not to buy.

Leskovee, Adamic, and Huberman (2007) concluded that eWOM is of great value in stimulating advertisements.

According to Cantallops and Salvi (2014), there are five main reasons why consumers would contribute reviews: self-directed, to help other consumers, social benefits, consumer empowerment, and to help companies. On the other hand, Casaló, Flavián, and Guinalíu (2010) found that consumers' intention to participate in online communities is dependent on the characteristics of the community. In other words, consumers are more likely to join online communities if they perceive them to be useful with an easy-to-use platform, which helps to develop a more positive attitude. In addition to Cantallops and Salvi's (2014) suggestion, Bronner and de Hoog (2010b) argue that consumer motivation is an influencing factor in the type of site consumers choose to visit. This motivation also drives the way consumers express themselves on review sites. Essentially, why, where, and what are the three "Ws" behind consumers' intention to contribute online.

Impact of CGC from the Consumer Perspective

Several studies (Lee, Park, and Han 2011; Papathanassis and Knolle 2011; Sparks and Browning 2011) explore the various reasons on how CGC can impact consumers' decision-making processes. Some results from these studies indicated that consumers perceive online reviews to be useful only when the "story" related in the reviews are on successes rather than on failures of a company's endeavor (Black and Kelley 2009). However, in Black and Kelley's (2009) study, they noted that consumers are more likely to give higher rating scores on helpfulness, when the story entails the company's effective recovery. On the contrary, Sparks and Browning (2011) found that consumers seemed to be more influenced by negative information, especially when the overall reviews are negative. However, when positive contextual reviews are paired with ratings, the level of consumer trust and purchase intention increases. In addition, Sparks and Browning (2011) found that when contextual reviews are positively framed, based on interpersonal service, the level of trust from consumer increases as well.

In terms of credibility, Xie et al. (2011) found that personal identifying information of reviewers increases the perceived credibility of online reviews. However, when such personal identifying information is paired with ambivalent reviews, consumers' intention to purchase a service or product decreases. Along with Xie et al. (2011) study, Loureiro and Kastenholz (2011) found that a company's reputation is a more significant determination of loyalty than consumers' satisfaction or delight. Although satisfaction and delight did not overpower the level of significance of reputation, these are the two distinct constructs in determining consumers' loyalty.

According to Hardey (2011), reliability is a factor that shapes purchasing behavior. CGC can be deemed credible when the reviews are based on experiences and opinions of real consumers (Xie et al. 2011). As mentioned in other studies, CGC needs to be a two-way communication in order to be effective. For example, TripAdvisor participates in CGC activity. The company reviews and responds to any specific consumers' review in an "equally open and visible fashion" (Hardey 2011, p. 762). Apart from reliability and credibility, indicators such as perceived trustworthiness, usefulness of CGC, and level of expertise (Black and Kelley 2009; Yacouel and Fleischer 2012) were also frequently referred to when there is a discussion on the effect of reviews on consumers' perspective. Papathanassis and Knolle (2011) claim that the risk reduction during the decision-making process is related to the purchase of intangible and inseparable service bundles. These perspectives inevitably affect consumers' decision-making process when consumers are trying to reduce the level of risk as much as possible (Kim, Mattila, and Baloglu 2011).

Gender also had a significant impact on consumers' motivation to read online reviews (Kim, Mattila, and Baloglu 2011). Similarly, Toh, DeKay, and Raven (2011) found that women are more active than men in terms of information search activities. In addition, research shows that the presence of CGC has a strong impact on product valuation and purchase decisions (Cantallops and Salvi 2014).

Another important indicator of the impact of CGC is related to the accessibility (Sparks and Browning 2011; Xiang and Gretzel 2010) and comprehensiveness of reviews. Cantallops and Salvi (2014) claim that consumers "have a complicated task filtering and analyzing" (p. 48) information written in reviews. These complications include influencing factors such as tone, valence, framing of the review (i.e., what is read first), and peripheral information such as star ratings. All this information adds up to influence the overall consumers' process of digesting the information they read through CGC.

Impact of CGC from the Company Perspective

Like CGC having an impact on consumers' perspective, it is also regarded a determining factor for a company's success. Several studies have analyzed the impact of CGC from the company's perspective (Dickinger 2011; Yacouel and Fleischer 2012), by considering company-generated content, its content quality in the online environment, and its possibility of interacting with clients and generating a price premium (Cantallops and Salvi 2014). Cantallops and Salvi (2014) determined seven main impact factors on consumer's perception of the company: generating loyalty; quality control and new procedures; revenue management; customer interactions, responses, and recovery; marketing strategies; target group communication; and online reputation comparison.

In addition, Loureiro and Kastenholz (2011) argued that corporate reputation has a significant impact on the customer's perspective of the service capability of the company. They explained that this perception leads to a reliable representation of the service the customer has in mind. Furthermore, in order to have a good idea of the company's service quality, customers often use several different resource platforms to search for more information. For example, Berthon et al. (2012) claimed that customers use direct company websites, official website cybermediaries, and customer review websites to evaluate the attributes of the company.

Other research found that with the increased number of communication platforms (Jahn and Kunz 2012; Toh, DeKay, and Raven 2011), companies are faced with both challenges and opportunities. With an array of new technological platforms available, consumers can compare the offerings of the same product from different companies based on prices or search for other alternatives within the same product category. Thus, for companies to compete for the same group of consumers, they need to establish a strong relationship with their targeted consumers.

Customer loyalty was a factor that was highlighted by CGC studies as well. Loureiro and Kastenholz (2011) measured customer loyalty using indicators such as intention to continue to buy the same product, repeated purchase, or willingness to recommend the product to others. However, Loureiro and Kastenholz (2011) found out that the degree of loyalty does not make a difference in consumers' repeated buying behavior if the consumer has already fallen into the loyal customer category.

The availability of social media has posed both risks and opportunities for companies. However, if the company is able to analyze any prevalent problems, these risks maybe converted into opportunities for the companies (Dickinger 2011). The ability to manage negative CGC (e.g., eWOM) is critical for consumers to stay competitive in the market. Some analyses conducted by companies who were faced with negative eWOM helped companies to improve their product or service quality, the identification of needs highlighted by their consumers, and the implementation of new policies (e.g., return policies) (Loureiro and Kastenholz 2011).

Positive eWOM on the one hand can help improve a company's positioning in the market. This competitive advantage could potentially allow consumers to change their pricing strategies (Yacouel and Fleischer 2012). However, if companies choose to ignore or address the negative comments, they could potentially dismiss consumers' interest, which can subsequently affect their pricing strategy and revenue generation.

eWOM, regardless of it being positive or negative, is important information for companies and their wellbeing. As Berthon et al. (2012) posit, CGC has a significant influence on companies' marketing strategies. eWOM is a CGC that can serve as a performance indicator for companies; companies can direct their energy toward a more profitable consumer segment, and they can also influence consumers' loyalty while retaining existing consumers.

Consumer Engagement in CGC

Communication between companies and consumers is no longer just an activity. Rather, it is just the beginning of consumer engagement in CGC. In fact, consumer involvement is no longer an option for companies; companies need to move a step ahead and start engaging their consumers in any marketing activities that they conduct, that is, consumer engagement.

Theoretical roots of the consumer engagement concept are referred to as the "expanded domain of relationship marketing" (Vivek, Beatty, and Morgan 2012, p. 129). Ashley et al. (2011) agree that relationship marketing is carried out through the examination of customer engagement. In the service industry context, Vargo (2009) refers to this notion as "a transcending view of relationships" (p. 378), which is the trend of the current consumer market. Companies can no longer survive in a goods-dominant marketplace. They are recognizing that the transcending relational perspective is consumer-centric or "other stakeholder's interactive experiences taking place in complex, co-creative environments" (Brodie, Hollebeek, and Smith 2011, p. 106), or both. It is important to realize that this transcendental relationship does not end with just the consumers. A firm's focus is on existing and potential customers, as well as the consumer communities and their "organizational value co-creative networks" (p. 106). Lusch, Vargo, and Tanniru (2010) suggest that interactive consumer experiences, which are cocreated with other players, can be regarded as the act of engaging. These co-creation experiences may range from product suggestion to product creation through CGC (e.g., feedback).

Definition of Consumer Engagement

The term "consumer engagement" has been defined differently by a few authors within the virtual brand community (Brodie, Hollebeek, and Smith 2011). Vivek, Beatty, and Morgan (2012) added that the definition differs throughout different disciplines. Thus, there is no agreement to whether one definition should be adopted over another. Consumer engagement may be described as the "intensity of an individual's participation and connection with the organization's offerings and activities initiated by either the customer of the organization" (p. 4). Customer brand engagement, on the other hand, refers to the "level a customer's motivational, brand-related and context-dependent state of mind characterized by specific levels of cognitive, emotional, and behavioral activity in brand interactions" (Hollebeek 2011, p. 6).

CGC platforms such as the SNS embeds the ideology for eWOM. SNS is practically the tool for consumers to freely create and disseminate product-related information on their established social networks. Be it image-based or text-based, consumers are subconsciously spreading the word about a product or service to friends, family, and other acquaintances through the great vine (Vollmer and Precourt 2008).

Depending on the age of media consumers, the preference for one social media over the other will vary. For example, according to Pew Research Center (www.pewinternet.org), half of the Internet users that were young adults (53 percent) ranging from 18 to 29 use Instagram. Also, for the first time, the number of LinkedIn Internet users with college education reached 50 percent. Based on Pew Research Center's Internet Project, social media usage ranking is as follows: Facebook (58 percent), LinkedIn (23 percent), Pinterest (22 percent), Instagram (21 percent), and Twitter (19 percent).

A social interaction engagement such as exchanging views on an opinion is not solely based on a consumer logging into an SNS. Rather, engagement includes some kind of social interactions, for example, commenting on a post or clicking "Like." By engaging in such interactions, consumers naturally exhibit their preferences for a product and services along with their persona (e.g., profile photo). This identification can stimulate online communication, which will eventually turn into eWOM. These days, eWOM is not only facilitated through company review websites, but they are also included in SNSs. This is because SNSs have developed over the years to facilitate such activity. As eWOM communications are regarded as CGC, marketing practitioners should gain a better understanding of the relationship between SNS users and the frequency of social media usage. There are many variables that underlie the social factors that influence consumers' engagement in the virtual world.

There is a lot of debate to whether eWOM is worth investigating. However, with changes in social media usage, it is fundamental for companies to investigate the cause of behavior (why and how). Furthermore, in order to stay competitive in the marketplace, it is essential for companies to understand the social relationship variables that affect consumers to be involved in CGC activity. Such understanding can help companies incorporate social media as an integral part of their marketing plan.

CHAPTER 3

Trustworthiness of Consumer-Generated Content

The motivation behind a consumer's desire to consume, participate, and produce all boils down to trust. When discussing electronic word-of-mouth (eWOM) in the social networking site (SNS) context, trust is a construct that cannot be ignored. In a classic academic literature, Hovland and Weiss (1951) argued that a communicator's trustworthiness is likely to influence a receiver's opinion about the source. This is not an uncommon relationship. For example, when we buy something online, if we do not trust a particular vendor, we will not be in a position to believe the claim expressed on the website. Reverting to the social media context, the higher the level of trust social media users have in their contacts, the higher is the possibility that they will engage in (1) opinion seeking, (2) contribution of opinion, and (3) the attitude for passing on opinions to others on SNSs. Thus, trust should be treated as an important means for consumers to evaluate the source and the value of the information. Trust can result in a halo effect in social media. For example, when a social media user establishes a level of trust with his social connections in his list of friends, the willingness to rely on those connections will be enhanced. This halo effect is largely due to the perceived trust and reliability, which will thereby increase consumer-generated content (CGC) behavior on these various SNSs.

Although credibility and validity have been topics of discussion since the birth of the Internet (Johnson and Kaye 2004), marketing academics are still discovering this area of interest (Sparks, Perkins, and Buckley 2013). Sen and Lerman (2007) noted that consumers are often confronted with a large volume of information when they use social media. In addition, this information is inconsistent with in itself, which causes a dilemma for these consumers during their decision-making process. Papathanassis and Knolle (2011) argued that consumers' perceptions, intentions, and decisions are not dependent only on its content but also on its presentation. These aspects of content and presentation include valence (Sparks and Browning 2011), informational cues (Hansen 2005), and source credibility (Brinol and Petty 2009). Furthermore, research has shown that in order for consumers to establish credibility and trust, organizations have to be responsive toward any comments written by their consumers (Revinate 2011). Being responsive is part of evaluating the value and reliability of both the positive and negative reviews.

According to Burgess et al. (2009), greater trust is placed on comments when they have a specific location (e.g., travel website) than when these comments are posted on a "generic social networking website" (p. 221). Consumers are constantly sourcing information using the Internet to aid in their decision-making process—particularly good experiences such as vacations and spa treatments. As these are considered "experience goods" and information about these experiences are not easily attainable. Thus, consumers tend to consult independent experts, salespersons, and fellow consumers.

Park, Lee, and Han (2007) categorize two types of product information for online consumers: seller-created and consumer-created. Seller-created information is available through the company's websites, whereas consumer-created information is available through a variety of social media platforms such as third-party websites (e.g., TripAdvisor), SNS (e.g., Facebook), and blogs. These consumer-created reviews have a dual capability—they not only provide useful information, but also serve as a recommender for that particular product.

In the online environment, CGC exchanges offer consumers an opportunity to share their experiences by posting their self-created content on the Internet. Burgess et al. (2011) argue that "there is typically far more information available to the consumer in the online environment from consumer-generated eWOM than from traditional WOM" (p. 223). The only barrier consumers have toward this vast amount of information online is their time and cognitive limits (Chatterjee 2001). Forums may serve as a vital resource when consumers are making their decisions; however, "forums do not always attract comments from typical consumers…it is more likely that consumers who have had extreme experiences are more likely to provide online comments or reviews" (p. 223).

Trust Perception by Different CGC Creators

Trust can be separated into two schools of thoughts: a belief or expectation, a behavior that reflects reliance on others, or uncertainty from the person who is triggering the trusting behavior (Chen 2006). Park, Lee, and Han (2007) argued that online consumer reviews are often viewed as more trustworthy and credible compared to company-generated information. Despite the argument that online reviews tend to be more trustworthy, there have been contradictory results when determining whether the information provided on corporate websites are more trustworthy than those reviews posted on general SNSs (e.g., Facebook) (Burgess et al. 2011). Independent, third-party type websites seem to be more favorable (e.g., fairly evaluated) among consumers (Ensing 2013). Nonetheless, while traditional forms of WOM tend to be from people who are known to consumers, online reviews are typically created by strangers, resulting in credibility concerns (Ensing 2013).

Research shows that one in four consumers thought that review site information is generally unfair (Ensing 2013). In addition, Ensing (2013) also found that consumers indicated skepticism by observing the rating site users. These users (60 percent) paid more attention to the actual consumer comments than to the numerical or star ratings accompanying the reviews. The reason these users focused on the textual comments is because they were trying to determine if the reviews were credible and whether these reviews were applicable to their own purchasing situations.

Park, Lee, and Han (2007) claim that information created by independent entities, such as government, regional, and industry-related websites, is a source perceived to allow elements of objectivity and credibility, and thus, deemed more reliable by consumers. Another source of information contributed by consumers is generic online forums. CGC tend to reflect threads of their purchasing experiences, views, and beliefs associated with the events in which they were involved. Furthermore,

Litvin, Goldsmith, and Pan (2008) posit that such CGC serves as a form of eWOM; it has been well accepted by the public and has even encouraged websites to include CGC platforms like weblogs, SNSs, and third-party websites in their website design.

Burgess et al. (2011) summarized different creators of online content in two or three main categories: independent expert (e.g., government websites), CGC (e.g., weblogs, SNS, and third-party websites), and seller-generated content (e.g., e-mail promotion based on the mailing list and seller's own website). All these content sources were tested for trustworthiness among consumers. The results show that the highest trust was afforded to information attained on the government websites. Burgess et al. (2011) argued that government websites are independent experts that understand the implications of trustworthy information and their responsibility in providing relevant and credible information to their consumers.

Surprisingly, Burgess et al. (2011) also found that the seller's websites were considered to be trustworthy, which contradicts previous research. They explained that perhaps the information provided on the website and questions were cohesive, therefore creating a basis for trust among consumers. Trust was also seen from consumers toward third-party websites such as TripAdvisor. The results suggest that the consumers tend to favor third-party websites over generic SNSs (e.g., Facebook) when consumers are looking for a specific product or service they intend to purchase. In addition, there were discussions that third-party websites have stricter control on the types of reviews posted. Burgess et al. (2011) added that defamatory postings will be compared less considerably to generic SNSs.

Moreover, they found that reviews posted on blogs and SNSs were the least trustworthy among consumers. An interesting finding from Burgess et al. (2011) was that consumers were not sure if they had visited a CGC site before. Despite having provided a definition in their study to their respondents, they assumed that these individuals might not have fully understood the concept of CGC. From their study, it shows that marketing practitioners could benefit by embedding a link of independent expert websites and third-party websites on their own website. Despite the popularity of SNSs (e.g., Facebook), it seems consumers are not prone to trust information that are posted on those sites. Burgess et al. (2011) also added that consumers are "more likely to trust consumer-created information" (p. 234) than those who had not visited a CGC site before.

Bazaarvoice's social trends report (2013) noted that in order for companies to maintain a strong relationship with consumers, they cannot just listen passively on social networks. "Brands must demonstrate that they're listening, and not just with friendly tweets from employees with no decision making power" (p. 19). Bazaarvoice gathered industrial experts and suggested that one way to show that the companies are responsive toward consumers' comments is to "make changes based on trends in feedback data" (p. 19). It is also important to note that when the changes are made, consumers should be informed of the changes—so that they know that they are being heard. By earning the appreciation from the consumers, they will feel compelled to contribute even more. A second suggestion to exhibit responsiveness is to simply respond to consumers' questions and feedback. Even if the feedback is negative, brands should warmly embrace it and not ignore it (p. 19).

Content of CGC

According to Petty and Cacioppo (1981), messages are designed to persuade readers by affecting both their beliefs and attitudes, which ultimately affects their behavior. They further elaborated that there are several elements in a message that contribute toward persuasion: content, source, contextual characteristics, and channel. Message content provides argument either for or against position, therefore influencing attitudes through belief formation (Petty and Cacioppo 1981). In a study conducted by Sparks, Perkins, and Buckley (2013), they argue that when consumers read reviews for an eco-resort, for example, they would expect message content to include commitment toward corporate social responsibility and environmental sustainability. Persuasion theory also assumes that beliefs and attitudes can be influenced by perceptions about the message source, including trustworthiness, credibility, and the recipient's beliefs about the source's intention to persuade (Petty and Cacioppo 1981). All these elements are essential in forming trust in the information provided (Sparks, Perkins, and Buckley 2013).

Based on Ajzen's (1991) attitude formation theory, attitude toward an object is based on a set of beliefs about that object, and those beliefs include perceptions of the "utility of the reviews, trust, quality" (Sparks, Perkins, and Buckley 2013). In addition, Sparks, Perkins, and Buckley (2013) suggested that positive attitudes and perceived trust in the reviews had the strongest association with purchase intentions. The second strongest correlation was the organization's credentials and quality.

When the credibility of sources for information becomes an issue, many consumers turn to news sites sponsored by traditional media. So, what does this mean? Has the level of confidence and faith for online sources declined? The question remains as to how much should consumers trust with their online information as part of their purchase decision-making process. Many consumers may argue that personal blogs are far more trustworthy than organization's sponsored website due to its candidness. Since company websites are motivated to sell, information stated on the it may be biased. However, on consumer-generated websites, it was also argued that not all information is accurate. The question is: How much faith should be placed on CGC?

Source Credibility Theory

Source credibility theory has been widely used in marketing and communication studies (Ayeh 2015). The source credibility perspective is expected to be relevant to the study of individual's use of information sources especially in the CGC context as there are many concerns in CGC, which hinge largely on credibility (Litvin, Goldsmith, and Pan 2008). In marketing, source credibility has been used to examine the effectiveness of endorsers in advertisement (Ayeh 2015), whereas, in communication studies, this theory is used to compare the credibility of media channels (Johnson and Kaye 2009). In addition, Watts and Zhang (2008) investigated the influence of source credibility as part of consumers' information adoption in online communities. More recent studies in various contexts have highlighted the effects of source credibility on various consumer behavioral outcomes such as purchase intentions, attitudes toward messages, and information adoption (Ayeh, Au, and Law 2013; Wang and Doong 2010).

In a study conducted by Ayeh (2015), the author found that credibility factors are antecedents of CGC's usefulness. Furthermore, both perceived trustworthiness and expertise yielded significant influence on usefulness perception. Trustworthiness and expertise were significant factors toward consumers' attitude toward using CGC as part of their decision-making processes. In other words, consumers are more "favorably disposed toward using" CGC for their decision-making processes (p. 178).

Source Trustworthiness

Ghazisaeedi, Steyn, and Van Heerden (2012) claim that source trustworthiness is a critical measure of the success of blog as a CGC platform. He argued that, generally, there are two avenues to understand the trustworthiness of the source: demographics of the source (blogger) and the demographics of the receiver (blog reader). Armstrong and Nelson (2005) had results showing that male authors were deemed more credible than female authors. Furthermore, supported by Xie et al. (2011), the authors confirmed that factors such as name, state of residence, and gender had a positive effect on the perceived credibility of the online reviews. However, Ghazisaeedi, Steyn, and Van Heerden (2012) found that trustworthiness was not related to gender ($p = 0.895$). On the contrary, age had a significant difference to source trustworthiness ($p = 0.01$). The authors used a post-hoc test to compare the age groups and found that source trustworthiness for blogs were significantly higher for the18 to 29 year old age group than the 40 to 49 year old age group. Results also showed that the education level did not have an impact on the source trustworthiness of the blogs (Ghazisaeedi, Steyn, and Van Heerden 2012).

Ghazisaeedi, Steyn, and Van Heerden (2012) found that the relationship between respondents' frequency on accessing blogs and the number of blogs respondents accessed were determining factors for source trustworthiness. In other words, light blog readers tend to be more skeptical about the credibility of the blogs compared to heavy blog users (Johnson and Kaye 2010).

Lothia, Donthu, and Hershberger (2003) found that the effectiveness of a blog is higher when the blogger is perceived to be trustworthy. However, the effectiveness of the blog decreases when there are advertisements present. In their study, they showed that "negative blog posts with no advertisement will be more effective than any other type of blog" (p. 317).

The Impact of CGC on Consumers' Trust

Early in the mid-1990s, the Internet has not gained much exposure. Consumers therefore assumed that the Internet was an outpost where discussion was readily available at no cost, and the contents of the post were blunt and frequently rebellious. When consumers lack knowledge on a particular product or service, there is always a high level of skepticism. Thus, it was suggested by several critics that the Web should be regarded as a less credible source of information than the traditional media. So why was the Web discriminated against having credible information? This is largely due to the nature of the Web. For those consumer-generated sites, the need for editorial sight was not enforced. In addition, majority of the consumer-generated sites created back then were sometimes created on a whim. There were no professional or social pressures to ensure that information posted was accurate and unbiased. As society is changing its culture with the introduction of the Internet, so is the attitude of individuals. Internet users back then were not fearful of criticism.

Although there were critics judging against the credibility of the Internet, there were also users who supported it. This attitude toward the Internet, however, is largely dependent on the frequency and comfort level of using the Internet. Some studies found that users who deem the Internet as a credible source of information indicated that they are frequent users who relied on the Internet for news and information.

CGC encompasses various platforms for WOM communication. WOM has historically remained the leading channel of communication that people trust and is a "go-to" source for many consumers. Although WOM is important and is one of the communication channels that many small businesses aim for due to lack of advertising expenses, the caveat is that negative news spread even faster than positive news.

On a global scale, 92 percent of consumers trusted words from their friends, family, and acquaintances (Nielsen Global Trust in Advertising and Brand Messages 2012). More specifically, according to the Global Trust in Advertising Report by Nielsen (2012), consumers tend to trust an advertisement if the information is delivered through recommendations from people they know. WOM has over 94 percent of consumers' trust in the Asia-Pacific region, 90 percent in the Middle East and Africa, 92 percent in Latin American, 89 percent in Europe, and 90 percent in the United States. As for the online environment, on a global average, consumers tend to find content mostly from the ads served in the search engine results, followed by 36 percent for online video ads, 36 percent for ads on social networks, and 33 percent for online banner ads. Within the North American population, ads served in search engine results were the most popular online ad formats (39 percent). The results suggest that there is a growing population with the online environment. Consumers are starting to see the relevance of the online information, which means that it is time for marketers to shift their focus to the online arena for their marketing strategies.

Challenges and Opportunities of CGC for Companies

With an increased activity on the virtual world and on the CGC on social media sites, companies are constantly keeping track on the "latest and greatest" trend on the market to keep their knowledge and position in the market up-to-date. At Google, searches for rating and reviews around consumer products have been growing (www.thinkwithgoogle.com). Marketing practitioners are no longer given an option to ignore this trend; rather they need to embrace it. Brett Hurt, Founder and CEO of Bazaarvoice, stated that most online ratings were between four and five stars. He claimed that the number one reason why people write content is altruism. This claim is backed up by a research conducted by Cheung and Lee (2012). They found out that "enjoyment of helping others is crucial in affecting consumers' eWOM intention" (p. 222). Cheung and Lee (2012) argued that the act of helping others can deter other community members from negative experiences as well as help others through their purchasing decisions. Professor Reibstein backs this point by stating that new research shows that people like to share good news more than bad (www.thinkingwithgoogle.com).

CGC pose as both a challenge and as an opportunity for companies. The challenge that is potentially harmful for companies is the constant introduction of new social media. Some companies deliberately create a "social media" department or communications department to have someone in-charge of the activities online. For example, updating Facebook account with updated information, responding to comments, addressing issues, and maintaining a strong relationship with current and potential customers. Twitter, Foursquare, and Yelp are some of the major CGC social media platforms. Another challenge is that CGC, when integrated with social media, has the power to spread the word fast and wide. This is a double-edge sword. Negative comments about a company's product or service can cause severe damage to the company if appropriate recovery is not done. Negative comments on Yelp have infamously caused companies, especially service-dominant companies, to fold their businesses. However, Kaushik, a Digital Marketing Evangelist at Google, pointed out that when there is a negative feedback, it is actually a great opportunity for companies to engage with the community and drive long-term brand engagement (www.thinkwithgoogle.com).

The positive note about being on social media is that the company will have a wider exposure in the market. Apart from their target market, any consumer who surfs the Internet could easily find out about the presence of a particular company. Flipping the Yellow Pages is no longer the route that consumers choose when looking for a service or company. In other words, researching on a company and or looking for a product and service is only a click away. In addition, positive comments will also have a positive impact on a company instantly.

Depending on the Social Technographics of the social media users, their personas will make a difference in what they wish to talk about online. For example, what are their interests and what are they passionate to share about? Looking at blogs, microblogs, image sharing sites, there are different types of comments, stories, and insights. It is vital for companies to be able to determine what their target audiences are passionate to talk about because it is the gateway to devise content that they will likely respond to.

Apart from knowing target audiences' interests, companies also need to understand how their customers talk to each other. In other words, companies need to know their "community" and devise a strategy to strengthen their relationship by participating in their conversations in a noninvasive manner. Marketing messages are therefore developed from these community conversations. Languages that are used in the messages need to be a familiar term for their target audience. There is no point using big words or expert terminology when it does not deliver the intended message. This is important for companies to build common ground with their target audience by acting like them.

When engaging in CGC, it is important that companies listen and respond to their target audiences. They also need to do their due diligence by researching on their competitors to keep current in the market as well as to maintain their competitive advantage. Another step to take is to create content and engage in conversations through different channels.

Impact of CGC on Consumer's Shopping Behavior

According to a recent report from Bazaarvoice (2015), CGC (e.g. online product reviews) has drastically changed the way consumers make their purchasing decisions. They found that there was a seasonal spike in using CGC in the food and beverage industry during the winter holiday season; While the automotive industry received an increase in CGC usage during the summer shopping season. Based on a worldwide survey, Bazaarvoice (2015) found that 71 percent of their respondents claim that CGC influenced their purchasing decision on a car. However, an incredible 88 percent of Australians claims that CGC had some influence on their purchasing decisions.

In the customer service industry, respondents noted that CGC is key in guiding their financial and service industry choices, but only 9 percent mentioned that banking reviews are a key service component for them.

Impact of CGC on Brands

Though marketers are encouraged to engage consumers and get them involved in the creativity of the ad developments, marketers must be sure to draw a line as to how they publicize this fact. As there are conflicting studies that find consumer-generated ads (CGA) to be more trustworthy than ads developed by professional firms, companies should strategize the engagement of CGC. For example, Doritos' engagement strategy was to first explain the origin of the consumer-generated ads to their target audiences. Then, a elaborated instruction was given to targeted audiences in regards to the steps involved if they (i.e. customers) want to be part of the collaborative effort. In addition, if a company were to engage in CGA, there should be a constant reminder of their strategic assessment of the brand's growth. In other words, they should be tracking the growth of their sales and not only relying on the power of CGA.

Although CGAs are effective in retaining a brand's loyal customers, they may not be effective for the long-term growth of the brand. Potential customers of the brand may not be as attracted to the ad as existing customers. Thus, marketers need to be aware of when to use CGAs, and when to use professionally created ads. They can assess their growth by evaluating their product lifecycle.

According to Steyn et al. (2011), CGAs are "increasingly impacting brand communication" (p. 58). However, there are conflicting results regarding the preference of company-generated ad over CGAs. In Steyn et al.'s (2011) study, their results showed that there was no significant effect found on whether CGAs were preferred over company-generated ads. However, they suspected that variables such as knowledge or perception of who created the ad, the popularity of the ad, and motivation for ad creation were impacted by "brand empathy and bonding" (Steyn et al. 2011, p. 58). A study by Lim, Chung, and Weaver (2012), on the other hand, discovered that CGC (e.g., videos) generated more views and comments compared to those that were generated by marketers.

According to Nielsen's Digital Consumer Report (2014), the content of the Internet, and who is creating it, is changing. In its latest tracking data on fast-growing Web sites, user-generated content sites (platforms for photo sharing, video sharing, and blogging) comprise 5 out of the top 10 fastest-growing Web brands. The popularity of these social sharing sites (e.g., Flickr, Instagram, Facebook) is driven by the content—which is consumer generated—and the desire to share information through a simple process of uploading photos through mobile devices (e.g., cellular phones). As the adage "a picture is worth a thousand words," it is much easier to view visual content on a small screen compared to reading the text. With eWOM, consumers are not only creating but also sharing their photos with each other and with the public (i.e., virtual community). As it is practically free, the benefits for participating and consuming in these activities are driven by the attitude toward using social media platforms as well as sharing of content. Largely due to viral marketing, CGC has been experiencing significant growth and marketers are taking advantage of such communication tools in their marketing strategies.

With the new consumption culture evolving around our lives, CGC has been experiencing dramatic traffic growth. It has gradually become a norm in our media consumption habits. Every type of CGC platform is competing with one other to attract more foot traffic. Starting with text-based CGC, slowly and gradually consumers are flocking toward using and creating visual CGC. For example, although YouTube has been the pioneer in online video, a rival video sharing site, Vimeo, seems to be expressing its dominance in the video sharing business. The main differences between these two video channels are content control and purposes of use (www.digitalebard.com).

CGC has definitely changed the way people search for information, learn about special topics, or enjoy themselves. It has a tremendous power that even politicians acknowledge. According to Shao (2008), it seemed like a norm for the U.S. 2008 Presidential candidates to advocate their candidacy through CGC social media such as YouTube. Let's take President Obama's Presidential campaign as an example. He was not only the first presidential candidate that used social media effectively. According to Rutledge (2013), Obama dominated the social media space because his team knew how to take advantage of the social media platforms. During that campaign, "Obama logged twice as many Facebook 'Likes' and nearly 20 times as many re-tweets as Romney" (mprcenter.org, para 5). Voters who needed more information about the candidate they are thinking of voting for can easily look up campaign materials. These interested voters not only find relevant information, but they can also create their own video materials to support their presidential candidates. CGC is indeed a social phenomenon that explains why people are drawn toward contributing to and using CGC social media.

Domingos (2005) argued that social network models are traditionally viewed as descriptive rather than predictive way of communicating a particular behavior. However, with the introduction of the Internet, the social network has been a hub where a large amount of information can be retrieved. This information is available on various social networks such as blogs, knowledge sharing sites (e.g., Epinions), collaborative filtering system, online gaming, newsgroups, and chat rooms.

Organizations often utilize positive WOM among customers to generate more profits. However, this also means that there should be more interactions among customers and the corresponding network effects similar to a traditional marketing model. CGC platforms, such as SNSs, have been a core tool for companies to capitalize on their profits. Companies establish a "network value" of customers. This network value is a formula that increases sales to others as a result from marketing to one customer. In other words, the network value of customers is a form of viral marketing, better known as WOM marketing. Such a marketing technique may lead to very suboptimal marketing decisions. Thus, companies are looking to target those customers with the highest network value, market to them, and reap the benefits of the ensuing wave of WOM.

Business Opportunities with CGC

As social media explodes and advances in our society, organizations are experiencing a power shift. The power shift currently is from organizations to consumers. In other words, consumers drive the trend of supply and demand especially in the retail industry. In order to capture the "hearts" of the consumers, several companies are engaged in CGC, also known as consumer-generated marketing (CGM). Having the power shifted toward the consumer is not a negative move. Which brand does not want its name to have more exposure with the generosity of consumers' time? For this reason, CGM is often heralded as a "dream come true" for many brands as that is the way to supersede their marketing agencies and get their advertising content out for free.

As we introduce new communication tools, brands realize that CGC might not be the best move if they want growth. It may be an ideal strategy if a brand wants high retention but might not be the best strategy for brand growth (www.forbes.com). This is because if consumers are the one in control of what goes out in the public, brands will lose their control and eventually post a potential risk for their brand more so if the content is not the greatest. Although CGC (e.g., consumer-generated videos) is an ideal money-saving technique, these contents may not be well executed and may be detrimental toward any creative strategy planned. The following are tips for companies to determine whether the use of CGC is appropriate for them. There are three scenarios that companies may consider to use CGC as part of their marketing and advertising campaign:

- Reinvention of a branded asset
- Offering rewards for creativity
- Storytelling

Reinvention of a Branded Asset

Sometimes the best source for new ideas and creativity is from consumers. Brands that have been experiencing stagnant growth may see a need to revitalize their brand name. Building upon existing equity and recognition in the elements of a brand is vital to maintain its position as the "top-of-mind" brand among consumers. Thus, one of the best ways is to get consumers involved and ask them for a fresh image, something that encompasses the intrinsic quality of a brand. For example, companies such as Folgers took advantage of their 25 year anniversary and asked their online population to participate in a re-recording of their famous theme song competition. The intrinsic component that was exemplified by the winner was the nostalgic feeling one would receive listening to the music; in other words, the purpose was to highlight the role that Folgers played in their lives.

Offering Rewards for Your Creativity

Coinciding with the Super Bowl event, Doritos hosted their annual "Crash the Super Bowl" contest for consumer-generated commercials. This type of CGC invites consumers to submit their original videos, photos, or stories, and the competition is based on their creativity. Doritos capitalized on this idea and have been airing their consumer-generated TV commercials during the Super Bowl period. Doritos' strategy to involve consumers has been very successful for the last few years. One of the main reasons for this success is the connection and relevance the CGC commercials have with the general public.

Another example of rewarding consumers for their creativity is through contests such as "Starbucks White Cup Art." Introducing contests not only enables consumers to add trust to the brand, but it also encourages higher consumer-engagement and enables consumers to have a better affinity to the brand. The winning consumers are rewarded by having their designs printed on a limited edition Starbucks reusable plastic cup.

GoPro is another company that also runs contests among its consumers. GoPro solicits cool videos from its consumers and rewards them by featuring their videos on GoPro's social media accounts.

Storytelling

An alternative to the above strategies is to have consumers share their stories. As the focus is on consumers and their interaction between other consumers as well as companies, the selling point of CGC is on storytelling. Storytelling is a business marketing space that may be referred to as content marketing (Figure 3.1). This method works for a majority of the brands out there. It requires a combined effort of carefully promoting and engaging consumers with the company's product(s). Content marketing "is the creation of valuable, relevant and compelling content by the brand itself on a consistent basis, used to generate a positive behavior from a customer or prospect of the brand" (Pulizzi 2012, p. 116).

Well-established companies such as Coca-Cola are showing that storytelling is at the center of new marketing today. Coca-Cola was aware of the shift in the marketplace and therefore saw a need for new

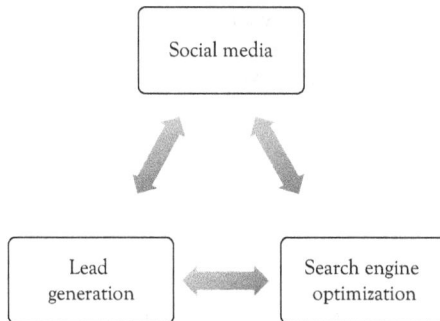

Figure 3.1 The storytelling mix

Source: Pulizzi (2012).

marketing techniques. Coca-Cola sees three shifts: consumer behaviors are changing online, companies are struggling to separate their messages from "technology" and SNSs such as Twitter, and there are opportunities for companies to develop deeper emotional connections with their consumers through storytelling (www.contentmarketinginstitute.com).

Regardless of whether a brand is searchable through search engine optimization (SEO) or through social media tools, none of these root sources will be effective if the brand is not accompanied by compelling story (Pulizzi 2012). In other words, as Pulizzi (2012) argued, technology tools do not serve a purpose "if content marketing strategy is not at the center of marketing" (p. 119). Google's Zero Moment of Truth found that consumers' purchasing decision is based on their engagement with online content. It was advised that the trend that leads toward high purchasing intention is to build a compelling story that allows consumers to engage in. Furthermore, Pulizzi (2012) posit that brands must ensure that their content is in the mix (Figure 3.1) while consumers' decisions are being made. Otherwise, companies will be left out of the content marketing practices entirely.

As discussed in the earlier chapters, facts and figures are no longer an attractive source among consumers. Rather, consumers are adopting the approach of empathizing with the story behind those creations. For example, in a recent study conducted by Moriuchi and Chung (2015), emotional messages such as storytelling were more effective as donation messages rather than statistical figures. In this research, the authors found that regardless of whether the donation is for domestic victims or international victims, an emotional message that tells a story is more persuasive than presenting the actual death toll of a natural disaster. Their results are intended to give charity organizations and non-profit organizations suggestions in regards to their solicitation strategy and marketing efforts towards their target market.

How to Stay Successful in the Market with Storytelling?

One of the biggest challenges that content creation expert Pulizzi (2012) pointed was the creation of engaging content. According to the Content Marketing Institute, a majority of the companies are struggling with creating content that can truly engage their customers and deliver results that benefit the company (www.contentmarketinginstitute.com). Thus, what makes great, not good, content? The suggestion provided by Pulizzi (2012) was based on the actual example created by Proctor and Gamble (P&G), "Home Made Simple"—targeting "Moms" on the go. Content that is regarded as great needs to be "targeted and have educational content portals" (p. 120). Essentially, marketers need to find a focus: a laser-like targeting strategy of a super niche category. As Pulizzi (2012) argued, the key success of P&G as a consumer-package leader was its strategy— they were very specific in their content, targeted to a specific buyer, and were relentless in their focus on useful and entertaining content, which engaged (truly) their readers and customers. On the contrary, the reason why companies are not successful in their content marketing is because the content is too broad.

Storytelling in the Consumer Market

Several organizations such as Copyblogger and Content Marketing Institute are embracing the roles of Chief Content Officer or Chief Storyteller. With the growing popularity of CGC platforms, content is being crated and distributed via several outlets. These outlets include social media, public relations, marketing, e-mail, marketing, mobile, and search engines (Pulizzi 2012).

In order to be sustainable in creating great content, Pulizzi (2012) commended the work of a company called OpenView Venture Partners. This company engages its employees in the content creation process with its customers. Currently, it has 90 percent of its employees blog on a regular basis—OpenView Labs, which is a major part of its content platform. Based on this content creation effort as part of the company's marketing plan, OpenView saw significant positive results: among others, a significant growth in sales, in site traffic, and over 10,000 opt-in subscribers in just 18 months.

Another tip that Pulizzi (2012) provided about a good storytelling technique is to remove the brand from the story. What this means is to "remove sales pitches entirely from the content to engender trust and credibility" (p. 122). Companies that successfully translated this tip into action were Adobe (CMO.com) and GE (Ecoimagination).

Lastly, Pulizzi (2012) posits that great content creation occurs when outside experts of that particular industry are included in the community. Their expertise will inevitably leverage the process of content creation. There have been several sites that offers industrial expertise and these sites are open to the public: Examiner.com, Copyblogger, as well as Content Marketing Institute. Being an Examiner writer myself, I am aware of the quality control that Examiner.com has on its writers. Subject experts are consulted and there is a quota to be met to ensure that new content is being contributed continuously. As part of the Copyblogger community, it was interesting and enriching for me to learn many techniques on content creation. Every so often, I receive e-mails on updates on content creation and trends being adopted by marketing practitioners at the moment.

The future of marketing will be heavily reliant on CGC, particularly, on content that is cocreated by the company and its consumers. The trend in marketing is leaning toward the model of half marketing and half publishing. Having consumers involved in a company's new product development is an activity of the past. Now, marketing practitioners are transitioning their marketing activities from "involvement" to "engagement." Engagement is no longer just a two-way communication; rather companies need to respond to real-time news as stories develop. Ultimately, marketing practitioners need to create, distribute, and capture their targeted audience—particularly a niche population—with valuable information. This does not only refer to co-creation, rather, to an engaging co-created value process.

The following are the five main factors that perhaps benefit first-time social media users, especially those who use SNSs as part of their business expansion. There are, of course, several factors that many marketing consultants would propose, but these five factors perhaps have a more direct impact on how successful a company (or even a sole proprietor) can be. In the following section, it is most appropriate to relate to Philip Kotler's mantra of marketing: CC-DV-TP. These acronyms stand for C: create, C: communicate; D: deliver, V: value; T: target audience,

P: profit. Social media marketing applies basic marketing principles but with an emphasis on the social media presence. Marketing experts (Kotler et al. 2002; Kotler 2012) highlighted that in planning a marketing strategy, it is important that we fulfill three basic activities: product management, brand management, and customer management. Using this model as a basis for a successful firm, and combining Plomion's (2014) five Cs of effective content marketing and Ernst's (2014) five C's in social media success in 2015, I incorporated both models into the following five factors to highlight the integration of social media into a marketing plan.

Factor 1: Creating

Content that is created needs to be of high quality and sensible. We live in a society with opinionated individuals. Thus, quality of writing alone is insufficient when relating the content to the public; rather, establishing a rapport with gatekeepers or other influencers may ultimately draw attention around the same topic. Nonetheless, the content posted has to be updated regularly to stay consistent with the current trends in the market.

Factor 2: Communicate

We are not only creating sensible and credible information; we are also communicating our intended message to our audience. We are communicating the value of our product and services offered, as well as our promise. This promise needs to hit three "buckets" of a consumer's thought process: cognitive, habitual, and affective.

Factor 3: Connect

Now that we have high-quality content and it links to relevant materials, what should we do next? Connect this information with your existing customers as well as your potential customers. We can reach and engage with consumers, influencers, and other like-minded leaders in the industry. This piece of information can be disseminated in several ways via several different social media. In a brick-and-mortar store, salesmen make sales calls face-to-face with their potential clients. Whereas, companies that are endorsing their social media presence will conduct these sales calls virtually. Ultimately, these businesses are following good business practices with integration of social media etiquette. However, despite the instant nature of social media, gaining fame or even recognition is not instant. We need to build our reputation with time. Thus, patience is required. As we build our connections with local communities and industries, we need to stay focused on our goals and objectives. Connection is a two-way street. We not only need to communicate our message to our intended audiences, we also need to listen and observe. Paying attention to our clients and addressing their concerns is part of enhancing the value and quality of our products and services.

Factor 4: Cross promote

In the virtual world, we cannot be lone rangers. We need to share our content across several different channels. Essentially, we need share our information on SNS platforms such as Facebook, Pinterest, Twitter, Instagram, or Google+. However, it is important to note that each SNS is unique in its own way. For example, Instagram is conducive to graphics more than just text, whereas Twitter is catered toward instant messages. Thus, customizing your content toward a particular platform is important as the way the intended message is sent maybe perceived differently. Also, relating back to a company's marketing strategy, we need to know our audience preferences. Does the target market comprise of business working professionals? If so, which platform is more popular among them? We need to ensure that we connect with our consumers with the appropriate platform.

Factor 5: Control

With any marketing strategy, there is always a need for control. With the amount of CGC flooding each social media, companies must be in control and ensure that the information posted or the information accepted is credible and trustworthy. Control is actually one of the challenges that companies are facing right now due to the flexibility and access of consumer contributed toward any social media. Thus, marketers need to consistently keep track of the content as well as update necessary information that is deemed time-sensitive. In fact, the control factor is the influencer in changing companies' image.

These five "Cs" are indispensable in ensuring that innovative technologies reach and engage consumers in the whole consumption process. However, it is important to note that no two communities are the same. Thus, some companies may feel that they need to emphasize more on a particular C than others, due to the nature of their product and services. This means that each company may require a somewhat customized approach. Hopefully, these five Cs can benefit and scale up to the maximum use of technology and contribute toward a positive experience for consumers alike.

CHAPTER 4

A Cross-National Perspective on Consumer-Generated Content

According to Brandtzæg (2010), culture influences lifestyle, and lifestyle influences the way individuals communicate and interact with new media technologies. Pookulangara and Koesler (2011) added that the social aspect of shopping "has ingrained in consumer culture for a long time" (p. 340). Culture has been effective in advertising, marketing strategies, and buying habits (Grier and Brumbaugh 1999). In this chapter, we will be discussing how culture affects the use and contribution of CGC.

There has been a rise in consumer-generated content (CGC) in recent years. However, very few studies investigate the attributes of CGC from a cross-national perspective. As Gretzel, Kang, and Lee (2008) indicate, regardless of whether there is a need to integrate CGC-related features on a website or to advertise on a consumer-generated third-party website, marketing practitioners need to first know the CGC "penetration and specific use behaviors associated with consumer-generated content in that specific market" (p. 101). Further, by gaining such an understanding, marketing practitioners will have a better idea of the technology diffusion of innovation in the market. It is also important to determine if the differences in adoption and use of CGC differs across markets. Kraemer, Gibbs, and Dedrick (2005) claim that when innovation is perceived differently and the acceptance of technology varies, there will be greater variation in innovation outcomes in different countries. Thus, it also means that consumers' adoption and use of CGC will differ across different nations.

As the consumer marketplace gradually places more reliance on the medium of digital communication, it is not surprising that a consumer develops the expectation that the presence of social media will have a great influence on the extent and type of use of an innovation, which has played the role of a communication medium. It has been argued that (Gretzel, Kang, and Lee 2008) CGC, especially in the form of media, requires certain technologies, technology ownership, Internet penetration, and broadband penetration. With an increasing number of consumers using the mobile platform for blogs and content creation, the goal of achieving convenience is even more demanding now.

According to Gretzel, Kang, and Lee (2008), in order to gain insights regarding the differences and similarities of CGC adoption and use, companies need to have an understanding of country-specific use behaviors, which are assumed to be driven and explained by cultural dimensions. In a collectivistic culture, group values and opinions of others are often deemed important. Asian cultures have been found to rely on more personal referral sources when purchasing products and services (Money, Gilly, and Graham 1998; Nielsen 2013). The difference between Asian websites and those in the West is that the former stresses on consumer–consumer interactivity, whereas the latter, which is highly individualistic, stresses on the marketer–consumer interactivity (Cho and Cheon 2005). Based on such an observation, CGC-related websites seem to foster interpersonal exchanges within social networks. Further, such CGC when embedded in websites is assumed to support the creation of communities, which are more likely to be used in the collectivistic cultures if they support social interactions. On the contrary, a highly individualistic culture such as the United States focuses on self-portrayal and self-presentation (Gretzel, Kang, and Lee 2008). CGC, which can be used to self-promote oneself, therefore suits the needs of an individualistic culture.

According to Sigala and Sakellaridis (2004), high power distance and masculine culture have a high preference for interactive websites. This suggests that Japanese and Chinese consumers are likely to have high levels of desire to interact with a website—coincidently a feature of CGC. On the other hand, Americans are likely to express their thoughts and place more emphasis on hedonic aspects of consumption (Malhotra and McCort 2001). This suggests that American consumers seek CGC websites to express themselves, and engage with content creation and content viewing for the sake of enjoyment (Gretzel, Kang, and Lee 2008).

Another cultural dimension, which discusses uncertainty avoidance, has been found to impact consumers' preferences for elaborative and substantial information on websites (Vishwanath 2004). Germans are considered on the high end of the spectrum for uncertainty avoidance. This means that Germans use CGC because of its high credibility and experiential bias (Gretzel, Kang, and Lee 2008) to complement information provided by marketer-generated websites. On the contrary, owing to their privacy concerns, this high uncertainty avoidance seems to be a barrier for Germans with regard to engagement with and active creation of CGC. In other parts of Europe such as in UK, people are known to enjoy conversations offline and thus are assumed to enjoy online discussions as well (Gannon-Leary and Fontainha 2007). According to Würtz (2005), China, with its high-context culture, seem to have a preference for visual information on websites. Thus, an image-based CGC can be assumed to be more popular with the Chinese than pure text-based CGC. The above discussion suggests that social networking sites (SNSs) will have a different role in each country as user experiences are dependent on the cultural dimensions of the country in which they are situated. Thus, it is important to understand the cultural dimensions of each respective country before deciding to use CGC as a part of the company's marketing strategy.

To further this discussion, we will examine three different cultural perspectives with examples of actual utilization of CGC. As a society is driven by cultural norms, individuals are pressured to exhibit certain behavior that might not necessarily be in their best interest. Three countries, United States, Japan, and Singapore, were chosen on the basis of their cultural orientation and their differences in attitude and acceptance of CGC.

Many online media consumers are likely to assume that all social media platforms are identical. This also means that social media companies adopt a standardized approach, also known as the etic perspective, when introducing social media to other countries outside of the United States. So, do any of the social media companies adopt a localized strategy (the emic perspective), for their social media platforms? In the following sections, we will explore the role of CGC in each of these countries.

United States of America

The United States is a country that values individualism, indulgence, and masculinity. Hofstede, a culture guru, explored the U.S. culture through the lens of his six dimensions and determined the driving forces behind American culture. It is important to note that these dimensions serve as a mental shortcut to obtain an overview of the country and do not generalize all Americans; everyone is unique. However, the presence of social norms generally ensure that most people to stay within the norm or better known as the so-called approval radius.

U.S. scores high on the individualism dimension: People are generally concerned about their self-image and define themselves as "I" rather than "we." This dimension also emphasizes that it is a norm for people to focus on themselves and their direct family. On the other end of the spectrum, collectivist societies encourage interdependence within a society. People on this end of the spectrum belong to the "in-groups" and maintain high loyalty to each other.

U.S. consumers are fairly active in online activities. Majority of the applications (also known as apps) on mobile devices have been created and developed by American entrepreneurs, including Facebook, Twitter, and Instagram, among others. If we look at online reviews as an example, there are more reviews on Amazon.com and eBay.com than other review sites.

Pew Research determined that as of January 2014, 74 percent of Internet users in the United States were engaged in SNSs. Among the online adult users of this population, it was found that Facebook had the most foot traffic (71 percent); LinkedIn and Pinterest were at a tie (28 percent); followed by Instagram (26 percent); and then Twitter (23 percent). All these social networking platforms are enjoying an increase in user engagement compared to the 2012 usage records (www.pewinternet.org).

Now, why are Americans so eager to use social media? First, we have to return to Hofstede's dimensions of American society. Americans are known to be individualistic; therefore they are more concerned about themselves as well as their direct family members. Smith (2011) claimed that Americans use the Internet to stay connected with their family members and friends. What other better way is there to connect with the people you care? The answer: social media. Of course, apart from staying in touch with current friends and family members, people are also eager to find their long-lost friends. Social media users who are primarily interested in reconnecting mostly belong to the 50 and under age group.

Is social media used just to reconnect with friends and stay in touch with current friends and family? No, there is more. A smaller percentage (14 percent) of the online adult users caught the social media bug because they want to connect with people who have the same hobby or interest (www.pewresearchinternet.org). These people generally fall into the middle-aged and older adult category. Interestingly, Pew Research found that men are more likely than women to connect on social media with regards to topics on hobby. The remaining users claimed that they used social media to make new friends (9 percent). The smallest population of social media users were just interested in reading comments from public figures (e.g., politics) or in finding romantic partners.

Japan

The Japanese, according to Hofstede's cultural dimension, is a collectivist society. Historically, Japanese feel the need to blend in with others and not stand out. The need for affiliation is one of traits of Japanese culture. However, as society changes and new consumption habits develop, Japanese individuals see the need for uniqueness more than affiliation. However, despite the shift in consumption behavior, Japanese are still not comfortable in expressing their feelings and thoughts in a public hemisphere. Even if they have to contribute their opinions, the content is often softened by the tone coupled with barely any negative words. On CGC review sites such as Rakuten, the population of reviewers is still minimal. However, CGC platforms, like the Japanese social media, are gaining popularity.

So, can SNSs sustain in the Japanese consumer environment? The answer is yes. During the my time living and working in Japan for several years, I observed train commuters engaging in online activities on their cellular devices. Owing to the long train commutes to school or work, many Japanese either choose to sleep or fidget with their mobile devices. Thus, as early adopters of mobile Internet population, most Japanese social networks were developed for mobile devices. Furthermore, as per the code of social etiquette in Japan, talking on cellular phones on public transportation is taboo. Thus, text-based communication is how many Japanese commuters choose to spend their time (rather than napping) while enduring lengthy commutes.

The nature of SNS and the social conformity practiced by Japanese society contradicts each other. Boosting and highlighting your success online is just not the way of life for Japanese. Hence, it has taken some time for social networks to gain popularity.

Japanese consumers have gradually increased their participation and activity in the virtual world. With the introduction of tablets and smartphones, the popularity of social media has increased. Facebook, Mixi (a Japanese social networking), and Twitter are some of the top social media forms. Contributions on Yelp or even reviews on Amazon. com or Rakuten have been increasing, but it appears that negative comments or reviews are not as prevalent as they are on U.S. websites. All these SNSs have gradually gained popularity as more and more Japanese people become aware of social media. I conducted interviews with some of her friends and acquaintances on their use of social media, and found that majority of the younger respondents were "hooked" onto the daily updates on Facebook. The popularity of Mixi has declined since the introduction of Facebook in Japan.

In a research conducted by Moriuchi and Takahashi (2015), they discovered that Japanese consumers are more likely to contribute a review when their trust toward the e-vendor is negative. Moriuchi and Takahashi (2015) explained that this unexpected finding is probably due to the Japanese culture of humility. In Japan, individuals are not comfortable with giving positive feedback. It was mentioned by Kopp (2013) that the Japanese consider giving praise as a form of sarcasm. The term used is *homegoroshi*, which literally means "to kill with compliment," and is used to describe this perception. In other words, positive feedback could be perceived to be effusive and negative. In a similar vein, Japanese consumers may not be motivated to compliment an e-vendor because he or she may perceive it as sarcasm instead of positive feedback.

Twitter

Another popular social media site is Twitter. Twitter launched its Japanese version in 2008 and Japanese users only comprise 9 percent of overall active Twitter users (www.socialmediatoday.com) at that time. The setup of Twitter compliments the culture of Japanese. Twitter allows users to remain anonymous online, and with its high regard for privacy, Japanese users feel less inhibited when they voice their opinions. Twitter is relatively casual and has an unusual freedom for users to vent anonymously about everything under the sun. The Japanese caught the Twitter bug on being influenced by Hollywood celebrities. In 2010, with the World Cup being the main attraction, Japanese users broke the tweeting record: Japanese users posted 3,283 tweets per second (blogs.wsj.com). To put it into perspective, when the Los Angeles Lakers won the NBA Championship, there was a record of 3,085 tweets per second (www.twitter.com).

The Twitter phenomenon is global, but Japan only caught up to it when the Japanese-language version was introduced in 2008, with a mobile version last October. According to Nielsen Online, the number of Internet visitors who engage in microblogging sites rose from an estimated 1.9 to 7.5 million in March since October. With Twitter's newfound fame in Japan, many people find Mixi (a Facebook equivalent) troublesome. The perceived etiquette was to maintain relationships on the SNS which can be daunting at times. Furthermore, Mixi has the ability to track digital footprints of visiting users to other's profiles. On account of their conformist culture, the Japanese feel obligated to acknowledge every form of communication, which would result in a never-ending round of virtual gratitude. Twitter, on the other hand, has a friendly image. Japanese users feel that on Twitter, they do not have to be bothered by every single communication posted. Rather, they can pick and choose what they want to pay attention to and what to ignore.

The word "tweeting," when translated, means mumbling. This definition has naturally created a perception of an informal method of communication. The main difference between Twitter and Mixi is that the former can be considered a mumbling forum, whereas the other is known as a private communication channel. Another reason for using

Twitter among the Japanese is the restricted number of characters. As compared to alphabets, the number of characters when typed in Japanese can convey a wholesome message.

Facebook versus Mixi

Even though Facebook may not have had as much buzz in Japan, it did create a new perceived environment for Japanese users. Facebook in Japan is now viewed as a platform where successful people in real life gather. These people were labeled as "ria-ju" (riaru jiujitsu), which means "real fulfillment." This is a popular word among teenagers in 2011 and has become very famous on Facebook. Facebook has also become a job-hunting platform for recent college graduates.

Mixi is the Japanese version of Facebook and has a longer standing history in SNSs in Japan. However, the introduction of Facebook has caused Mixi's member registration and activity to decline. Recently, Mixi has been witnessing tremendous growth, which could be due to the success of an in-app game called "Monster Strike." Other SNSs that have a presence among Japanese users are Mobage, Pinterest, Instagram, and SnapChat.

Singapore

Geographically, Singapore is a part of the South-East Asia region. It belongs to the Association of Southeast Asian Nations (ASEAN) and is part of the Asia-Pacific Region (APAC). ASEAN is an organization of countries that is geographically located in Southeast Asia, and is established to promote cultural, economic, and political development in the region. This organization was officially formed in August 8, 1967, with the signing of the ASEAN Declaration (www.asean.org).

Singapore is a unique country based on its history. Due to the British colonization, Singapore follows the British system for education, governance, and infrastructure. Most importantly, Singapore has adopted English as its official language. However based on the demographics of Singapore, which is similar to the United States in terms of diversity, it is a melting pot and trading hub for the neighboring Asian countries.

Singapore citizens, also known as Singaporeans, have thus developed a westernized social identity despite their ethnic Asian background. Singapore is a rather modernized country that amalgamates Asian and Western cultures. Singapore is considered here in this study due to its uniqueness. Singaporeans, just like the Americans, are very proactive in developing new apps and innovations, and have high participation in online activities. I lived in Singapore for more than 10 years. For the purpose of this book, I interviewed my contacts in the country, regarding Singaporean's adaptation to online activities.

According to hashmeta.com, Singaporeans are one of the most active social media consumers in the world. Based on infographics about social media usage in Singapore, Singaporeans' use of social media is extensive and can be expected to evolve continuously. The total population of Singapore in 2013 was recorded at 5.4 million, of which 4 million are users of the Internet (aseanup.com). This is an estimated 86 percent of Internet penetration. According to aseanup.com, the e-commerce market in Singapore was estimated at US$3.08 billion and mobile commerce was estimated at US$1.2 billion. It was recorded that Singapore was ranked eighth for Internet penetration worldwide and fourth in Asia. In regards to Singaporeans' digital activities, majority of online communication comprised e-mail use, reading online news, searching for information, instant messaging, and social networks. Singaporeans are also fairly active with video streaming, and this is evident at the level of college education at the national universities of Singapore. Podcasting and other types of video streaming are often used as a part of the curriculum.

Word-of-mouth via SNSs greatly influence Singaporeans in their purchasing decisions. According to aseanup.com, Singaporeans (42 percent) use SNS when researching products, and 51.2 percent make decisions based on SNS and community forums. With their active participation in online activities, it is not unusual to see the boom in the e-commerce sector in Singapore. With an increase in mobile device sales as well as in mobile device usage, it is not surprising that online shopping skyrocketed (US$3.1 billion), with traveling and resort bookings amounting to US$307 million (28 percent). It was also reported that Singaporeans shop on overseas websites such as Amazon (62.6 percent) primarily because of product availability, greater choice, lower price, better discounts, and most importantly, the Singaporean dollar is strong against other foreign currency.

In Singapore, Facebook is the most popular social media platform (wearesocial.sg). For B2B social marketing, LinkedIn and Facebook were ranked the most preferred social media platforms to use. Twitter is the second most popular SNS in Singapore capturing 54 percent of the social media users. Google+ (45 percent) was third in popularity, followed by LinkedIn (36 percent), and lastly Instagram (25 percent). According to the Google trend, Instagram has overtaken Twitter as the second most popular SNS (54 percent) in Singapore. Interestingly, similar to the Americans, 46.2 percent of Singaporeans are active on social media sites, often as the go-to source for product reviews, user experiences, and comments (www.hashmeta.com).

Social media has not only been used as a resource for consumers' purchasing decision-making for Singaporeans; it has also expanded its circle of usage by sharing consumers' social behavior in public. According to CityLab (www.citylab.com), Singaporeans are hooked on the Internet for spreading awareness toward shameful behavior. I learned about "stomping" through my brother who lives in Singapore. I conducted more secondary research on this topic since there is more to learn about this phenomenon. An online portal known as Straits Times Online Mobile Print (STOMP), owned by Singapore's top newspaper company, *The Straits Times*, is a social media site that allows consumers to upload photos and videos of "bad" behavior. Singapore has gained the reputation of upholding righteous behavior, best known for its attempt to control behavior by punishing people for vandalism or imposing death penalty for some drug offenses. Interestingly, instead of challenging the government for monitoring the public, Singaporean STOMPers (those who rattle on their fellow consumers) join the government in highlighting bad behaviors. These STOMPers outwardly post pictures with captions to describe bad behaviors in public. Some of the themes that emerged in recent posts on STOMP (www.stomp.com.sg) were substandard hygiene, ill-mannered foreigners, and "bad" behaviors on public transportation (www.citylab.com).

Now, the question is, how influential is this social media site? According to the editors at STOMP, in 2013, this social media site had a total of

1.2 billion page views and 18 million unique visitors. These outstanding results led STOMP to receive the first place for "Best in Online Media" at the 2013 Asian Digital Media Awards. There were several debates on whether STOMPing your fellow peers is a benefit or an additional stress to the community. On one hand, citizens are trying to create a better living environment for everyone and contribute matters that are of concern and importance to them. However, on the other hand, every little matter gets publicized, which may cause inconvenience to their peers. Essentially, the activity of STOMPing is regarded a double-edge sword and Singaporeans sees this as a debatable topic. Apart from STOMP, an online portal known as The Online Citizen, was also developed to encourage Singaporeans to openly criticize state policies.

CHAPTER 5

Optimizing Consumer-Generated Content

Today, everything is about the Internet, social media, and the power to tell an engaging story about a brand on consumer-generated content (CGC) platforms. It is arguable that a company may be considered as a "laggard" and not an "innovator" if it is not a part of any social network. Regardless of the type of social media platforms (Facebook, YouTube, Pinterest), if a company is not an active participant of these cyberspaces, they may lose the competitive edge compared to their major competitors. CGC platforms allow firms to engage with their consumers in a timely manner. This form of communication is not only cost-effective, but it also provides a higher level of efficiency, which may not be necessarily obtained through traditional communication tools. Thus, social media inevitably plays a major role in large, medium, and small firms at international and domestic levels. It is important to note that not all social media platforms are beneficial. Depending on the nature of the product and the target market, companies may wish to strategically select social media outlets that are beneficial to them. Regardless of the type of social media platform used—which involves CGC—there are three zones of return on investment (ROI) that companies may want to focus on.

The Three Zones of ROI for CGC

According to a *Huffington Post* article (www.huffingtonpost.com), Hayes (2015), Vice President of Bazaarvoice, argued that consumers these days have the option to shop whenever and wherever they want—online, in-store, on their mobile devices, and so on. Furthermore, consumers are migrating from brick-and-mortar shopping to the digital retail environment. However, in the digital environment, shoppers cannot gain a hands-on experience with the product they wish to purchase. Thus, these consumers turn to online reviews—looking at like-minded consumers' opinions on a product. These reviews, also known as CGC, are available in various formats and platforms, from photos and videos on social media to product reviews on review websites. Such CGC plays a valuable role in creating a better shopping experience for consumers who shop in a digitally driven environment. Based on a report by Bazaarvoice, there are three distinct zones that will benefit companies: conversion, search engine optimization (SEO), and product insights on their ROIs.

Zone 1: Conversion

According to Bazaarvoice, reviews are a proven sales driver. The reason why reviews have an impact on sales is because they serve as a validation tool for consumers who have a purchasing intention for product(s) that they wish to consider. Reviews are even more important when money is scarce, which makes decision-making harder. This relates to a theory known as the prospect theory, which discusses the gains and losses of a consumer's decision-making process. For example, if a decision is weighted to be a loss than a gain, then the decision will not be made. When companies are not active in soliciting reviews, they will notice a difference in the amount of traffic through their website, which could be essentially translated into sales. Nonetheless, even with just one review, companies will see a "10 percent lift in orders, and that number jumps to 30 percent with the accumulation of 50 reviews" (www.huffingtonpost.com, para 2).

There is a chain effect when it comes to the number of review volume. The more product reviews, the more page views, which in turn increases consumer purchase (www.huffingtonpost.com). According to Hayes (2015), when the number of reviews increases, there will be a steep incline in conversion rates, and these increments will continue to increase well past 1,000 reviews. However, it is important to note that the conversion benefits of reviews are more prevalent and immediate during the early stage of its volume growth.

Zone 2: Search Engine Optimization

SEO favors fresh content (Hayes 2015). In fact, based on Google Analytics, freshness of content is one of Google's five factors in algorithm update, which explains why SEO experts are constantly preaching the importance for new, relevant materials on a regular basis. Despite the importance of fresh content, the average product page on a website is filled with old content—"100 words in both the header and the footer and 150 words of product description" (Hayes 2015, para 5)—which is the opposite of being an SEO-friendly page.

It is perhaps a challenge for companies to regularly update their product features and relevant materials. A solution to such a challenge is to incorporate reviews on a product page, which can transform the way the pages appear on search engines. Companies take advantage of consumer reviews and reap the SEO benefits by incorporating a small number of product reviews. Hayes (2015) suggests using a mere eight reviews with an approximately 800 words of CGC and reducing the amount of duplicate content from "57 percent to a palatable 17 percent and increases the total product-specific content to 83 percent of the page" (Hayes 2015, para 6).

When unique page content increases, the number of reviews per page rises as well. This is important because search engines such as Google place emphasis on unique and relevant content. Relevant and unique content available on product page(s) is just as important as fresh content posted on product pages.

Based on the algorithm of Google Analytics, the higher the volume of reviews on a regular basis, the fresher the product page and content diversity. With a better grasp over SEO, companies are attracting more reviews which have more in-depth content (i.e. informative) to be indexed by search engines. According to Bazaarvoice, the addition of reviews to a product category page typically results in a "15 to 25 percent increase in search traffic" (Hayes 2015). This implies that even a mere number of reviews can contribute towards business equity.

Zone 3: Product Insights

Hayes (2015) suggested that an implementation of reviews on websites and product pages will result in immediate ROI. Hayes (2015) also pointed out that as soon as a product accumulates a minimum of 100 reviews, companies will see some exciting results. Furthermore, a company benefits additionally when its product reaches at least 100 reviews because this volume of review is large enough to conduct a deeper analysis on consumers' product sentiments and brand opinions. Consumer reviews are intended to provide direction for improvements within existing products or for new innovative products. Volume is particularly important in this zone since there is a need to have a large sample size of reviews to allow for a more accurate understanding of customer needs and wants.

Businesses aspire to obtain five-star reviews across all of their product categories and services. However, it is important to note that narrative (i.e. written comments) reviews of any star rating can offer important hints toward product insights. According to Hayes (2015), products reviews with one- to three-star ratings generally provide most content around product flaws and shortcomings. Whereas products with three- to four-star ratings often serve as a good source for product suggestions. Within the three- to four-star rating reviews, terms such as "however" and "only if" are indications of a shift in tone, which should be carefully analyzed. Not all pivotal language is an indication of a problem. Some may merely be suggestions for improvement or opportunities to connect with customers.

Another advantage of a heavily reviewed product for companies is that it helps establish patterns for fraud reviews. Hayes (2015) highlighted that almost 48 percent of consumers believe that one or more reviews displayed on a product review page is fake. Thus, companies should detect fraudulent reviews based on those existing review patterns and work to eliminate those overarching fraud trends to help maintain and build consumer trust in the brand.

Regardless of the shopping activity occurring on a particular mobile device or a social media platform, or even in a brick-and-mortar store, the role of different CGC, such as reviews, is important in consumers' decision-making process. This role will only grow as the years go by. Brands and companies should take advantage of consumers' reliance on CGC by driving additional review submissions and engagement, and realizing the full ROI of their network. Hayes (2015) argued that from a business perspective, when a network uses content that is generated from within the network (i.e., people using the product and service), these reviews are there to "offer powerful insights into the pulse of entire industries" (para 10). Such CGC will benefit both old and new, big and small entities as these companies evaluate their ongoing marketing strategies for the future. With just the knowledge of CGC and its new prominent role in marketing plans, the next important step is to understand how to develop persuasive content for the marketing plan.

As storytelling becomes the next big marketing technique, companies are readily tapping into consumer's emotions when marketing their content to their consumers.

The Future of CGC

The future of CGC plays an important role and its importance is linked to content creation and co-creation by both companies and consumers. Acuzno (2015) claims that most organizations embrace the powerful blend of different types of technologies and hence the impact of technique will become a bigger priority in the near future. As suggested by Hayes (2015), majority of product content is contributed by consumers (i.e., CGC); thus marketers should realize that CGC will play a key role in content marketing for companies. Being first and the loudest is not the way to go; rather companies should hire, train, and promote individuals who are capable of being creative and prolific in combining both the consumers' comments and company's goal.

Acuzno (2015) noted that content marketing requires a certain level of craftsmanship. Thus, automating everything because of technological barriers or lack of enthusiasm to learn how to be creative will end up hurting a company's own cause. Ultimately, great content marketers start with the examination of the circuitry of what makes content great.

Most importantly, to fully utilize CGC in a good content marketing plan, companies must have the right mentality. Acuzno (2015) introduced the SEED approach, which stands for Skills, Examples, Excitement, and Drive. This approach is where the scale (scaling of content) is about consistency, quality, experimentation and testing, and better, deeper connections to more consumers. In addition, Acuzno (2015) claims that this SEED approach comprises essential elements of great content creation. Once the page visits increase, it is an indication that the marketers have mastered the quality output and are reaching their goals of both serving their consumers and converting them.

Hampton et al. (2011) claim that there is an increased profound influence in the way an average Internet user consumes information. This influence is CGC, which is shared through personal blogs, social network-ing sites (SNS), online communities, discussion boards, product reviews, travel sites, YouTube videos, Instagram photo sharing, and many more. "Entire industries are being transformed" (McDonald 2010, para 1). For example, the retail and travel industries will never be the same again.

Based on market research, 81 percent of people use consumer reviews in their purchase decision for electronics, 77 percent for appliances, and 70 percent for books (Nielsen 2013). These were the top three new product categories ranked by the percent of people who claimed that the Internet is an important resource in their decision-making process. Furthermore, online reviews are second only to WOM when it comes to influencing purchasing decision (Anderson 2012).

Back in 2006, Nielsen claimed that the percentage of CGC contribu-tors was still small based on the overall Internet population. Furthermore, those who contribute are young. Furuthermore, Johnson (2012) added that although the rule-of-thumb was noted years ago, this Internet cul-ture still hold truth till this day. Variants of this Internet culture include the 90-9-1 principle where 90 percent of the participants of a commu-nity only view the online content, 9 percent edit the content, and only a mere 1 percent will actually actively create new content and contrib-ute to online platforms (Chen, Wang, and Li 2014). Bazaarvoice (2015) reported that young and affluent individuals (ages 25 to 34) use CGC the most (54 percent). On a global scale, 87 percent of the respondents who earned $150,000 and above indicated that CGC has influenced their decision for one of their offline purchases. CGC contributors are still growing, and CGC will continue to have a significant impact on con-sumers' decision-making process, especially when such content becomes a part of the company's content marketing strategy. Despite the advantages of using CGC in content marketing, there are also some critical chal-lenges that companies face. These challenges include managing the grow-ing mass of CGC and the quality of these voices (e.g., product reviews).

CGC Best Practices

With the diffusion of CGC in content marketing, there are promising way of resolving CGC challenges. For example, major e-commerce vendors, social media, and SNS provide options to readers to flag objectionable comments for removal. Efforts were also made to block comments that committed repeated offences (e.g., violation of site standards). Website owners also exercise caution with the use of anonymous comments. One of the ways to validate credibility is to make it mandatory for members to be registered on the site, which forces them to identify themselves—one such consumer review site is Angie's list. Other consumer review sites like Yelp uses a proprietary algorithm that gives more prominent placement to "established" community reviews (McDonald 2010).

Major newspapers are also moving away from letting commenters stay anonymous. For example, *The Washington Post* plans to revise its comments policy to ensure commenters use their real names. *The New York Times* also requires people to register before they can comment on a post. *The Huffington Post* website plans to include changes such as ranking commenters based on how well other readers know and trust their writing.

Interestingly, when reviews are posted on Amazon.com, those comments that are deemed most helpful are often written under real names (McDonald 2010). "Subscriber only" comments are also one of the popular features introduced by *The Wall Street Journal.* This feature allows a reader to choose from anonymous to subscriber-written comments.

CGC is advancing to the next level among major e-commerce vendors, social media, and SNSs. It has not only become a part of a company's content marketing strategy, it is in fact leading the way of how consumers receive, participate, and contribute information. For example, movie goers' use Rotten Tomatoes (www.rottentomatoes.com), a community site, to discover movie ratings before they decide to watch one in the theater or rent one for home entertainment. This CGC community site is a prime example of how a product review site uses the total package of "filtering sorting, reputation scores, site activity, community policing, member profile information, and its own proprietary algorithms" (McDonald, 2010, para. 20). All these precautions are exercised to ensure that the information posted is validated and that movie lovers can participate according to their level of comfort.

The future of CGC is tremendous for consumers and brands. However, to deal with the massive amount of content produced by consumers, what is needed now are new methods to filter all information according to relevance, reputation, and accuracy. Without such filtration, CGC would be just a collection of "noise" that consumers may no longer rely on in the future.

Last Thoughts

Consumers engage in an emotional activity when they are consuming online content. In the process, different parts of the emotional spectrum are engaged—fear, interest, happiness, surprise, and so on. CGC is different from traditional advertising, which attempts to involve the target audience at an emotional level. The difference between CGC used by companies (i.e., content marketing) and traditional marketing is the element of trust. CGC is about winning consumers' trust first, then dealing with their emotions. Typical commercials often tug at our heartstrings, which can be quite pitch-centric at times. Furthermore, with the presence of permission marketing, consumers can choose to use ad blocks or simply ignore the advertised messages and treat them as noise. As Kumar (2015) argues, CGC is the future for a company's content marketing strategy. However, Kumar (2015) stressed that using CGC as a part of a company's marketing strategy should not "look like marketing to earn the opportunity to nurture their interest in your product" (Kumar 2015, para 7). Essentially, companies need to know when to do the right thing at the right time.

References and Bibliographies

Aarts, H., and A. Dijksterhuis. 2000. "Habits as Knowledge Structures: Automaticity in Goal-Directed Behavior." *Journal of Personality and Social Psychology* 78, no. 1, pp. 53–63.

Abelson, R.P., and D.A. Prentice. 1989. "Beliefs as Possessions: A Functional Perspective." In *Attitude Structure and Function*, eds. A.R. Pratkanis, S.J. Breckler, and A.G. Greenwald, pp. 361–81. England: Lawrence Erlbaum Associates.

Acuzno, J. June 25, 2015. "The Future of Content Creation Requires Humans Not Robots." Content Marketing Institute. http://contentmarketinginstitute.com/2015/06/future-content-creation/

"Advertising Ecosystem." n.d. Interactive Advertising Bureau. www.iab.net/data/ecosystem.html

Aiken, L.S., and S.G. West. 1991. *Multiple Regression: Testing and Interpreting Interactions*. Thousand Oaks, CA: Sage.

Ajzen, I. 1991. "The Theory of Planned Behavior." *Organizational Behavior and Human Decision Processes* 50, no. 2, pp. 179–211.

Ajzen, I. 2006. "Constructing a Theory of Planned Behavior Questionnaire." TPB Questionnaire Construction, pp. 1–12. http://people.umass.edu/aizen/pdf/tpb.measurement.pdf

Anderson, S.P. 2007. "Regulation of Television Advertising." In *The Economic Regulation of Broadcasting Markets*, eds. P. Seabright and J. von Hagen, pp. 189–224. United Kingdom: Cambridge University Press.

Anderson, M. March 12, 2012. "Study: 72% of Consumers Trust Online Reviews as Much as Personal Recommendations." http://searchengineland.com/study-72-of-consumers-trust-online-reviews-as-much-as-personal-recommendations-114152

Armstrong, C.L., and M.R. Nelson. 2005. "How Newspaper Sources Trigger Gender Stereotypes." *Journalism and Mass Communication Quarterly* 82, no. 4, pp. 820–37.

Ashley, C., S.M. Noble, N. Donthu, and K.N. Lemon. 2011. "Why Customers won't Relate: Obstacles to Relationship Marketing Engagement." *Journal of Business Research* 64, no. 7, pp. 749–56.

Ayeh, J.K. 2015. "Travellers' Acceptance of Consumer-Generated Media: An Integrated Model of Technology Acceptance and Source Credibility Theories." *Computers in Human Behavior* 48, pp. 173–80.

Ayeh, J.K., N. Au, and R. Law. 2013. "Predicting the Intention to Use Consumer-Generated Media for Travel Planning." *Tourism Management* 35, pp. 132–43.

Bandura, A. 2001. "Social Cognitive Theory: An Agentic Perspective." *Annual Review of Psychology* 52, no. 1, pp. 1–26.

Bargh, J.A., K.Y. McKenna, and G.M. Fitzsimons. 2002. "Can You See the Real Me? Activation and Expression of the 'True Self' on the Internet." *Journal of Social Issues* 58, no. 1, pp. 33–48.

Bazaarvoice. 2014. "Social Trends Report 2014." http://media2.bazaarvoice.com/documents/Bazaarvoice_WP_SocialTrendsReport-2014.pdf

Bazaarvoice. 2015. "The Conversation Index." (Volume 9). http://media2.bazaarvoice.com/documents/Bazaarvoice-Conversation-Index-9-DIGITAL.pdf

Bazaarvoice's Social Trends Report. 2013. http://resources.bazaarvoice.com/rs/bazaarvoice/images/Bazaarvoice_Social-Trends-Report-2013.pdf

Bentham, J. 1982. *An Introduction to the Principles of Morals and Legislation.* eds. J.H. Burns and H.L.A. Hart, p. 343, London: Methuen.

Berridge, K., and P. Winkielman. 2003. "What Is An Unconscious Emotion? (The Case for Unconscious "Liking")." *Cognition and Emotion* 17, no. 2, pp. 181–211.

Berthon, P., M.B. Holbrook, J.M. Hulbert, and L. Pitt. 2007. "Viewing Brands in Multiple Dimensions." http://sloanreview.mit.edu/article/viewing-brands-in-multiple-dimensions/

Berthon, P., L. Pitt, and C. Campbell. 2008. "Ad Lib: When Customers Create the Ad." *California Management Review [P]* 50, no. 4, pp. 6–30.

Berthon, P.R., L.F. Pitt, K. Plangger, and D. Shapiro. 2012. "Marketing Meets Web 2.0, Social Media, and Creative Consumers: Implications for International Marketing Strategy." *Business Horizons* 55, no. 3, pp. 261–71.

Bizrate Insights. October 16, 2012. "Pinterest vs. Facebook: Which Social Sharing Site Wins at Shopping Engagement?" *PR Newswire.* www.prnewswire.com/news-releases/pinterest-vs-facebook-which-social-sharing-site-wins-at-shopping-engagement-174407851.html

Black, H.G., and S.W. Kelley. 2009. "A Storytelling Perspective on Online Customer Reviews Reporting Service Failure and Recovery." *Journal of Travel and Tourism Marketing* 26, no. 2, pp. 169–79.

Blackshaw, P. 2008. *Satisfied Customers Tell Three Friends, Angry Customers Tell 3,000: Running a Business in Today's Consumer-Driven World.* New York: Crown Business.

Blackshaw, P., and M. Nazzaro. 2006. "Consumer-Generated Media (CGM) 101: Word-of-Mouth in the Age of the Web-Fortified Consumer." New York: Nielsen BuzzMetrics.

Bortree, D. 2005. "Presentation of Self on the Web: An Ethnographic Study of Teenage GirlsgeWeblogs." *Education, Communication and Information* 5, no. 1, pp. 25–39.

Bowman, S., and C. Willis. 2003. *We Media: How Audiences Are Shaping the Future of News and Information.* Reston, VA: The Media Center at the American Press Institute.

Brandtzæg, P.B. 2010. "Towards a Unified Media-User Typology (MUT): A Meta-Analysis and Review of the Research Literature on Media-User Typologies." *Computers in Human Behavior* 26, no. 5, pp. 940–56.

Briggs, J. 2014. "How Do Users Interact with SERPs On Mobile Devices?" *Briggsby.* www.briggsby.com/how-do-users-interact-with-serps-on-mobile-devices/

Brinol, P., and R.E. Petty. 2009. "Source Factors in Persuasion: A Self-Validation Approach." European Review of Social Psychology 20, no. 1, pp. 49–96.

Brodie, R.J., L.D. Hollebeek, and S.D. Smith. June 14–15, 2011. "Engagement: An Important Bridging Concept for the Emerging SD Logic Lexicon." Paper presented at University of Auckland Business School 2011 Naples Forum on Service, Naples.

Bronner, F., and R. de Hoog. 2010a. "Vacationers and eWOM: Who Posts, and Why, Where, and What?" *Journal of Travel Research* 50, no. 1, pp. 15–26.

Bronner, F., and R. de Hoog. 2010b. "Consumer-Generated Versus Marketer-Generated Websites in Consumer Decision Making." *International Journal of Market Research* 52, no. 2, pp. 231–48.

Bryant, J., and J. Davies. 2006. "Selective Exposure to Video Games." In *Playing Video Games: Motives, Responses, and Consequences*, eds. P. Vorderer and J. Bryant, pp. 181–96. Mahwah, NJ: Erlbaum.

Bughin, J.R. 2007. "How Companies Can Make the Most of User-Generated Content." *McKinsey Quarterly*, pp. 1–4.

Bughin J., J. Doogan, and O.J. Vetvik. 2010. "A New Way to Measure Word-of-Mouth Marketing." *McKinsey Quarterly*, April. McKinsey and Company. www.mckinsey.com/insights/marketing_sales/a_new_way_to_measure_word-of-mouth_marketing

Burgess, S., C. Sellitto, C. Cox, and J. Buultjens. June 2009. "User-Generated Content (UGC) in Tourism: Benefits and Concerns of Online Consumers." In *17th European Conference on Information Systems*, pp. 417–29. Vienna.

Burgess, S., C. Sellitto, C. Cox, and J. Buultjens. 2011. "Trust Perceptions of Online Travel Information by Different Content Creators: Some Social and Legal Implications." *Information Systems Frontiers* 13, no. 2, pp. 221–35.

Byers, J.W., M. Mitzenmacher, and G. Zervas. 2012. "The Groupon Effect on Yelp Ratings: A Root Cause Analysis." In *Proceedings of the 13th ACM Conference on Electronic Commerce (EC)*, pp. 248–65. New York, NY.

Campbell, C., L.F. Pitt, M. Parent, and P.R. Berthon. 2011. "Understanding Consumer Conversations Around Ads in a Web 2.0 World." *Journal of Advertising* 40, no. 1, pp. 87–102.

Cantallops, A.S., and F. Salvi. 2014. "New Consumer Behavior: A Review of Research on eWOM and Hotels." *International Journal of Hospitality Management* 36, pp. 41–51.

Carpenter, S. 2000. "Effects of Cultural Tightness and Collectivism on Self-Concept and Causal Attributions." *Cross-Cultural Research* 34, no. 1, pp. 38–56.

Casaló, L.V., C. Flavián, and M. Guinalíu. 2010. "Determinants of the Intention to Participate in Firm-Hosted Online Travel Communities and Effects on Consumer Behavioral Intentions." *Tourism Management* 31, no. 6, pp. 898–911.

Chan, K.W., and S.Y. Li. 2010. "Understanding Consumer-to-Consumer Interactions in Virtual Communities: The Salience of Reciprocity." *Journal of Business Research* 63, no. 9, pp. 1033–40.

Chatterjee, P. 2001. "Online Reviews: Do Consumers Use Them?" *Advances in Consumer Research* 28, no. 1, pp. 129–33.

Chen, C. 2006. "Identifying Significant Factors Influencing Consumer Trust in an Online Travel Site." *Information Technology and Tourism* 8, no. 3–4, pp. 197–214.

Chen, C.P. 2013. "Exploring Personal Branding on YouTube." *Journal of Internet Commerce* 12, no. 4, pp. 332–47.

Chen, J., W. Geyer, C. Dugan, M. Muller, and I. Guy. April 2009. "Make New Friends, but Keep the Old: Recommending People on Social Networking Sites." In *Proceedings of the SIGCHI Conference on Human Factors in Computing Systems*, pp. 201–10. New York, NY: ACM.

Chen, G., X. Wang, and X. Li. 2014. *Fundamentals of Complex Networks: Models, Structures and Dynamics*. Singapore: John Wiley & Sons.

Cheung, C.M., and M.K. Lee. 2012. "What Drives Consumers to Spread Electronic Word of Mouth in Online Consumer-Opinion Platforms." *Decision Support Systems* 53, no. 1, pp. 218–25.

Cheung, C.M., M.K. Lee, and N. Rabjohn. 2008. "The Impact of Electronic Word-of-Mouth: The Adoption of Online Opinions in Online Customer Communities." *Internet Research* 18, no. 3, pp. 229–47.

Chevalier, J.A., and D. Mayzlin. 2006. "The Effect of Word of Mouth on Sales: Online Book Reviews." *Journal of Marketing Research* 43, no. 3, pp. 345–54.

Cho, C.H., and H.J. Cheon. 2005. "Cross-Cultural Comparisons of Interactivity on Corporate Web Sites: The United States, the United Kingdom, Japan, and South Korea." *Journal of Advertising* 34, no. 2, pp. 99–115.

Cho, S., and J. Huh. 2010. "Content Analysis of Corporate Blogs as a Relationship Management Tool." *Corporate Communications: An International Journal* 15, no. 1, pp. 30–48.

Chu, S.C., and Y. Kim. 2011. "Determinants of Consumer Engagement in Electronic Word-of-Mouth (eWOM) in Social Networking Sites." *International Journal of Advertising* 30, no. 1, pp. 47–75.

Clary, E.G., M. Snyder, R.D. Ridge, J. Copeland, A.A. Stukas, J. Haugen, and P. Miene. 1998. "Understanding and Assessing the Motivations of Volunteers: A Functional Approach." *Journal of Personality and Social Psychology* 74, no. 6, pp. 1516–30.

Cohen, N. 2007. "A History Department Bans Citing Wikipedia as a Research Source." *New York Times*, February 21. Retrieved from November 10, 2014. www.nytimes.com/2007/02/21/education/21wikipedia.html?pagewanted= print&_r=0

comScore Network. May 4, 2006. "694 Million People Currently Use the Internet Worldwide According to comScore Networks." www.comscore.com/ Insights/Press-Releases/2006/05/comScore-Launches-World-Metrix

Constantinides, E., and S.J. Fountain. 2008. "Web 2.0: Conceptual Foundations and Marketing Issues." *Journal of Direct, Data and Digital Marketing Practice* 9, no. 3, pp. 231–44.

Constantinides, E., C.L. Romero, and M.A.G. Boria. 2009. "Social Media: A New Frontier for Retailers?" In *European Retail Research*, pp. 1–28. New York: Springer.

Conway, J.C., and A.M. Rubin. 1991. Psychological Predictors of Television Viewing Motivation. *Communication Research* 18, no. 4, pp. 443–63.

Danescu-Niculescu-Mizil, C., G. Kossinets, J. Kleinberg, and L. Lee. April 2009. "How Opinions Are Received by Online Communities: A Case Study on Amazon.com Helpfulness Votes." In *Proceedings of the 18th International Conference on World Wide Web*, pp. 141–50. New York, NY: ACM.

Daugherty, T., M.S. Eastin, and L. Bright. 2008. "Exploring Consumer Motivations for Creating User-Generated Content." *Journal of Interactive Advertising* 8, no. 2, pp. 16–25.

Daugherty, T., M.S. Eastin, L.F. Bright, and S.C. Chu. 2011. "Expectancy-Value: Identifying Relationships Associated with Consuming User-Generated Content." In *Digital Media and Advertising: User Generated Content Consumption*, eds. M.S. Eastin, T. Daugherty, and N.M. Burns, pp. 146–60. New York: Information Science Reference.

Daugherty, T., E. Matthew, and H. Gangadharbatla. 2005. "E-CRM: Understanding Internet Confidence and Implications for Customer Relationship Management." In *Advances in Electronic Marketing*, pp. 67–82. Hershey, PA: Idea Group Publishing.

Dellarocas, C. 2003. "The Digitization of Word of Mouth: Promise and Challenges of Online Feedback Mechanisms." *Management Science* 49, no. 10, pp. 1407–24.

DeMers, J. 2013. "The Top 7 Social Media Marketing Trends that will Dominate 2014." www.forbes.com/sites/jaysondemers/2013/09/24/the-top-7-social-media-marketing-trends-that-will-dominate-2014/

DeMers, J. September 23, 2014. "The 6 Main Types of Blog Post and How to Use them." www.forbes.com/sites/jaysondemers/2014/09/23/the-6-main-types-of-blog-posts-and-how-to-use-them/

DeMers, J. January 2, 2014. "How User-Generated Content Will Shape Marketing in 2014." www.huffingtonpost.com/jayson-demers/how-user-generated-content_b_4533000.html

Dev, C.S., J.D. Buschman, and J.T. Bowen. 2010. "Hospitality Marketing: A Retrospective Analysis (1960–2010) and Predictions (2010–2020)." *Cornell Hospitality Quarterly* 51, no. 4, pp. 459–69.

Dickinger, A. 2011. "The Trustworthiness of Online Channels for Experience- and Goal-Directed Search Tasks." *Journal of Travel Research* 50, no. 4, pp. 378–91.

Dimmick, J., Y. Chen, and Z. Li. 2004. "Competition Between the Internet and Traditional News Media: The Gratification-Opportunities Niche Dimension." *The Journal of Media Economics* 17, no. 1, pp. 19–33.

Domingos, P. 2005. "Mining Social Networks for Viral Marketing." *IEEE Intelligent Systems* 20, no. 1, pp. 80–82.

Dominick, J.R. 1999. "Who Do You Think You Are? Personal Home Pages and Self-Presentation on the World Wide Web." *Journalism and Mass Communication Quarterly* 76, no. 4, pp. 646–58.

Droge, C., M.A. Stanko, and W.A. Pollitte. 2010. "Lead Users and Early Adopters on the Web: The Role of New Technology Product Blogs." *Journal of Product Innovation Management* 27, no. 1, pp. 66–82.

Duan, W., B. Gu, and A.B. Whinston. 2008. "Do Online Reviews Matter?—An Empirical Investigation of Panel Data." *Decision Support Systems* 45, no. 4, pp. 1007–16.

Duggan, M., N.B. Ellison, C. Lampe, A. Lenhart, and M. Madden. January 9, 2015. "Social Media Update 2014." *Pew Research Center*. www.pewinternet.org/2015/01/09/social-media-update-2014/

Dwyer, C. 2007. "Digital Relationships in the 'Myspace' Generation: Results from a Qualitative Study." In *System Sciences HICSS 2007, 40th Annual Hawaii International Conference on*, p. 19. Washington, DC: IEEE Computer Society.

Eastin, M.S., and T. Daugherty. 2005. "Past, Current, and Future Trends in Mass Communication." In *Marketing Communication: Emerging Trends and Developments*, pp. 23–40. United Kingdom: Oxford University Press.

eBizMBA Inc. March 2015. "Top 15 Most Popular Social Networking Sites." www.ebizmba.com/articles/social-networking-websites

Elliott, N. October 1, 2013. "The Social Technographics Score Helps Marketers Create Better Social Strategies." http://blogs.forrester.com/nate_elliott/13-10-01-the_social_technographics_score_helps_marketers_create_better_social_strategies

Ellison, N.B. 2007. "Social Network Sites: Definition, History, and Scholarship." *Journal of Computer-Mediated Communication* 13, no. 1, pp. 210–30.

Ellison, N.B., and D. Boyd. 2013. "Sociality Through Social Network Sites." In *The Oxford Handbook of Internet Studies*, ed. W.H. Dutton, pp. 151–72. Oxford: Oxford University Press.

Ellison, N.B., C. Steinfield, and C. Lampe. 2011. "Connection Strategies: Social Capital Implications of Facebook-Enabled Communication Practices." *New Media and Society* 13, no. 6, pp. 873–92.

Ensing, D. July 2013. "Research White Paper: Customer Rating and Reviews Site: An Up and Coming Crisis of Conflict." *Maritz Research*. www.maritzresearch.com/~/media/Files/MaritzResearch/Whitepapers/Customer-Rating-and-Reviews-Site_rev.pdf

Ernst, J. December 18, 2014. "The 5 C's of Social Media Success for 2015." http://smync.com/the-5-cs-of-social-media-success-for-2015/

Ertimur, B., and M. Gilly. 2010. "The Impact of Consumer-Generated Advertising on Brand Associations." *Advances in Consumer Research* 37, pp. 286–87.

Fang, Y., I. Qureshi, H. Sun, P. McCole, E. Ramsey, and K.H. Lim. 2014. "Trust, Satisfaction, and Online Repurchase Intention: The Moderating Role of Perceived Effectiveness of E-commerce Institutional Mechanisms." *Mis Quarterly* 38, no. 2, pp. 407–27.

Fazio, R.H., and T. Towles-Schwen. 1999. "The MODE Model of Attitude-Behavior Processes." In *Dual Process Theories in Social Psychology*, pp. 97–116. New York: Guilford Press.

Fazio, R.H., and C.J. Williams. 1986. "Attitude Accessibility as a Moderator of the Attitude–Perception and Attitude–Behavior Relations: An Investigation of the 1984 Presidential Election." *Journal of Personality and Social Psychology* 51, no. 3, pp. 505–14.

File, T., and C. Ryan. November 2014. "Computer and Internet Use in the United States: 2013." American Community Survey Reports. www.census.gov/content/dam/Census/library/publications/2014/acs/acs-28.pdf

Fishbein, M., and I. Ajzen. 1975. *Belief, Attitude, Intention and Behavior: An Introduction to Theory and Research*. Reading, MA: Addison-Wesley.

Fishburn, P.C. 1968. "Utility Theory." *Management Science* 14, no. 5, pp. 335–78.

Flaherty, L.M., K.J. Pearce, and R.B. Rubin. 1998. "Internet and Face-to-Face Communication: Not Functional Alternatives." *Communication Quarterly* 46, no. 3, pp. 250–68.

Flanagin, A.J., M.J. Metzger, R. Pure, A. Markov, and E. Hartsell. 2014. "Mitigating Risk in Ecommerce Transactions: Perceptions of Information Credibility and the Role of User-Generated Ratings in Product Quality and Purchase Intention." *Electronic Commerce Research* 14, no. 1, pp. 1–23.

Flavián, C., M. Guinalíu, and R. Gurrea. 2006. "The Role Played by Perceived Usability, Satisfaction and Consumer Trust on Website Loyalty." *Information and Management* 43, no. 1, pp. 1–14.

Fletcher, D. August 18, 2009. "A Brief History of Wikipedia." *Time*. http://content.time.com/time/business/article/0,8599,1917002,00.html

Funk, T. 2009. *Web 2.0 and Beyond: Understanding the New Online Business Models, Trends, and Technologies*. Westport, CO: Praeger.

Galloway, A.R. 2012. *The Interface Effect*. Cambridge: Polity.

Gannon-Leary, P., and E. Fontainha. 2007. "Communities of Practice and Virtual Learning Communities: Benefits, Barriers and Success Factors." *eLearning Papers*, no. 5.

Gefen, D., and P. Pavlou. 2006. "The Moderating Role of Perceived Regulatory Effectiveness of Online Marketplaces on the Role of Trust and Risk on Transaction Intentions." *ICIS 2006 Proceedings*, Paper 81.

Gentile, B., J.M. Twenge, E.C. Freeman, and W.K. Campbell. 2012. "The Effect of Social Networking Websites on Positive Self-Views: An Experimental Investigation." *Computers in Human Behavior* 28, no. 5, pp. 1929–33.

Ghazisaeedi, M., P.G. Steyn, and G. Van Heerden. 2012. "Trustworthiness of Product Review Blogs: A Source Trustworthiness Scale Validation." *African Journal of Business Management* 6, no. 25, pp. 7498–508.

Ghose, A., and P. Ipeirotis. 2009. "The EconoMining Project at NYU: Studying the Economic Value of User-Generated Content on the Internet." *Journal of Revenue and Pricing Management* 8, no. 2, pp. 241–46.

Ghose, A., P.G. Ipeirotis, and B. Li. 2012. "Designing Ranking Systems for Hotels on Travel Search Engines by Mining User-Generated and Crowdsourced Content." *Marketing Science*, 31, no. 3, pp. 493–520.

Gillmor, D. 2008. *We the Media: Grassroots Journalism by the People, for the People*. Sebastopol, CA: O'Reilly Media, Inc.

Global Faces and Networked Places. March 2009. "A Nielsen Report on Social Networking's New Global Footprint." www.nielsen.com/content/dam/corporate/us/en/newswire/uploads/2009/03/nielsen_globalfaces_mar09.pdf

Godes, D., and D. Mayzlin. 2004. "Using Online Conversations to Study Word-of-Mouth Communication." *Marketing Science* 23, no. 4, pp. 545–60.

Graber, D.A. 1993. *Mass Media and American Politics*. 4th ed. Washington, DC: Congressional Quaterly.

Gretzel, U., and K.H. Yoo. 2008. "Use and Impact of Online Travel Reviews." *Information and Communication Technologies in Tourism* 2008, pp. 35–46.

Gretzel, U., M. Kang, and W. Lee. 2008. "Differences in Consumer-Generated Media Adoption and Use: A Cross-National Perspective." *Journal of Hospitality and Leisure Marketing* 17, no. 1/2, pp. 99–120. doi:10.1080/10507050801978240

Grewal, R., R. Mehta, and F.R. Kardes. 2000. "The Role of the Social-Identity Function of Attitudes in Consumer Innovativeness and Opinion Leadership." *Journal of Economic Psychology* 21, no. 3, pp. 233–52.

Grier, S.A., and A.M. Brumbaugh. 1999. "Noticing Cultural Differences: Ad Meanings Created by Target and Non-Target Markets." *Journal of Advertising* 28, no. 1, pp. 79–93.

Grisham, J.R., R.O. Frost, G. Steketee, H.J. Kim, A. Tarkoff, and S. Hood. 2009. "Formation of Attachment to Possessions in Compulsive Hoarding." *Journal of Anxiety Disorders* 23, no. 3, pp. 357–61.

Gummerus, J., V. Liljander, E. Weman, and M. Pihlström. 2012. "Customer Engagement in a Facebook Brand Community." *Management Research Review* 35, no. 9, pp. 857–77.

Gupta, P., and J. Harris. 2010. "How e-WOM Recommendations Influence Product Consideration and Quality of Choice: A Motivation to Process Information Perspective." *Journal of Business Research* 63, no. 9, pp. 1041–49.

Hahn, W. January 8, 2013. "Vimeo vs. YouTube – Key Differences Between Two Top Video Channels." www.digitalbard.com/vimeo-vs-youtube-key-differences-between-two-top-video-channels/

Hampton, K.N., L.S. Goulet, L. Rainie, and K. Purcell. June 16, 2011. "Social Networking Sites and Our Lives: How People's Trust, Personal Relationships, and Civic and Political Involvement Are Connected to Their Use of Social Networking Sites and Other Technologies." *Pew Research Center.* www.pewinternet.org/files/old-media/Files/Reports/2011/PIP%20-%20Social%20networking%20sites%20and%20our%20lives.pdf

Hanna, R., A. Rohm, and V.L. Crittenden. 2011. "We're All Connected: The Power of the Social Media Ecosystem." *Business Horizons* 54, no. 3, pp. 265–73.

Hansen, T. 2005. "Perspectives on Consumer Decision Making: An Integrated Approach." *Journal of Consumer Behaviour* 4, no. 6, pp. 420–37.

Hardey, M. 2011. "To Spin Straw into Gold? New Lessons from Consumer-Generated Content." *The International Journal of Market Research* 53, no. 1, pp. 13–15.

Harmon-Jones, C., B.J. Schmeichel, and E. Harmon-Jones. 2009. Symbolic Self-Completion in Academia: Evidence from Department Web Pages and Email Signature Files." *European Journal of Social Psychology* 39, no. 2, pp. 311–16.

Hashmeta. n.d. "Social Media in Singapore 2014 [Infographic]." www.hashmeta.com/social-media-singapore-infographic/

Hayden, B., and R. Tomal. October 22, 2012. "A History of Social Media [Infographic]." www.copyblogger.com/history-of-social-media/

Hayes, A. 2015. "The 3 ROI Zones of Consumer-Generated Content." *The Huffington Post*, January 21. www.huffingtonpost.com/amy-hayes/the-3-roi-zones-of-consum_b_6510358.html

Head, A.J., and M.B. Eisenberg. 2010. "How Today's College Students Use Wikipedia for Course-Related Research." *First Monday* 15, no. 3.

Heinonen, K. 2011. "Consumer Activity in Social Media: Managerial Approaches to Consumers' Social Media Behavior." *Journal of Consumer Behaviour* 10, no. 6, pp. 356–64.

Hendrickson, M. July 24, 2007. "Nine Ways to Build Your Own Social Network." http://techcrunch.com/2007/07/24/9-ways-to-build-your-own-social-network/

Hennig-Thurau, T., C. Wiertz, and F. Feldhaus. 2014. "Does Twitter Matter? The Impact of Microblogging Word of Mouth on Consumers' Adoption of New Movies." *Journal of the Academy of Marketing Science* 43, no. 3, pp. 1–20.

Hennig-Thurau, T., K.P. Gwinner, G. Walsh, and D.D. Gremler. 2004. "Electronic Word-of-Mouth via Consumer-Opinion Platforms: What Motivates Consumers to Articulate Themselves on the Internet?" *Journal of Interactive Marketing* 18, no. 1, pp. 38–52.

Hoffman, D.L., and T.P. Novak. 1996. "Marketing in Hypermedia Computer-Mediated Environments: Conceptual Foundations." *The Journal of Marketing* 60, no. 3, pp. 50–68.

Hollebeek, L. 2011. "Exploring Customer Brand Engagement: Definition and Themes." *Journal of Strategic Marketing* 19, no. 7, pp. 555–73.

Hollenbaugh, E.E. 2010. "Personal Journal Bloggers: Profiles of Disclosiveness." *Computers in Human Behavior* 26, no. 6, pp. 1657–66.

Horrigan, J.A. 2008. "Online Shopping." *Pew Internet & American Life Project Report*, 36.

Hovland, C.I., and W. Weiss. 1951. "The Influence of Source Credibility on Communication Effectiveness." *Public Opinion Quarterly* 15, no. 4, pp. 635–50.

Hu, M., and B. Liu. August, 2004. "Mining and Summarizing Customer Reviews." In *Proceedings of the 10th ACM SIGKDD International Conference on Knowledge Discovery and Data Mining*, pp. 168–77. New York, NY: ACM.

Hu, Y., and S.S. Sundar. 2010. "Effects of Online Health Sources on Credibility and Behavioral Intentions." *Communication Research* 37, no. 1, pp. 105–32.

Humphreys, A., and K. Grayson. 2008. "The Intersecting Roles of Consumer and Producer: A Critical Perspective on Co-Production, Co-Creation and Prosumption." *Sociology Compass* 2, no. 3, pp. 963–80.

Hung, K.H., and S.Y. Li. 2007. "The Influence of eWOM on Virtual Consumer Communities: Social Capital, Consumer Learning, and Behavioral Outcomes." *Journal of Advertising Research* 47, no. 4, p. 485.

Interactive Advertising Bureau. April 2008. "IAB Platform Status Report: User Generated Content, Social Media and Advertising—An Overview." www.iab. net/media/file/2008_ugc_platform.pdf

Investopedia. n.d. "IPO Lock-Up." www.investopedia.com/terms/i/ipolockup.asp

Jahn, B., and W. Kunz. 2012. "How to Transform Consumers into Fans of Your Brand." *Journal of Service Management* 23, no. 3, pp. 344–61.

Jeong, E., and S.S. Jang. 2011. "Restaurant Experiences Triggering Positive Electronic Word-of-Mouth (eWOM) Motivations." *International Journal of Hospitality Management* 30, no. 2, pp. 356–66.

Johnson, B. May 6, 2012. "Is the 1% Rule Dead? The BBC Thinks So, but It's Wrong." https://gigaom.com/2012/05/06/bbc-1-percent-rule/

Johnson, B.K., and S. Knobloch-Westerwick. 2014. "Glancing Up or Down: Mood Management and Selective Social Comparisons on Social Networking Sites." *Computers in Human Behavior* 41, pp. 33–39.

Johnson, M.S., E. Sivadas, and E. Garbarino. 2008. "Customer Satisfaction, Perceived Risk and Affective Commitment: An Investigation of Directions of Influence." *Journal of Services Marketing* 22, no. 5, pp. 353–62.

Johnson, T.J., and B.K. Kaye, September 2004. "Wag the Blog: How Reliance on Traditional Media and the Internet Influence Credibility Perceptions of Weblogs among Blog Users." *Journalism and Mass Communication Quarterly* 81, no. 3, pp. 622–42, doi:10.1177/107769900408100310

Johnson, T.J., and B.K. Kaye. 2009. "In Blog We Trust? Deciphering Credibility of Components of the Internet Among Politically Interested Internet Users." *Computers in Human Behavior* 25, no. 1, pp. 175–82.

Johnson, T., and B. Kaye. 2010. "Choosing is Believing? How Web Gratifications and Reliance Affect Internet Credibility Among Politically Interested Users." *Atlantic Journal of Communication* 18, no. 1, pp. 1–21.

Joyce, E., and R.E. Kraut. 2006. "Predicting Continued Participation in Newsgroups." *Journal of Computer-Mediated Communication* 11, no. 3, pp. 723–47.

Kaplan, A.M., and M. Haenlein. 2010. "Users of the World, Unite! The Challenges and Opportunities of Social Media." *Business Horizons* 53, no. 1, pp. 59–68.

Kaplan, A.M., and M. Haenlein. 2011. "The Early Bird Catches the News: Nine Things You Should Know About Micro-Blogging." *Business Horizons* 54, no. 2, pp. 105–13.

Katz, E., and P.F. Lazarsfeld. 1995. "Between Media and Mass/the Part Played by People/the Two-Step Flow of Communication." In *Approaches to Media*, eds. O. Boyd-Barrett and C. Newbold, 124–34. London: Arnold.

Katz, E., J. Blumer, and M. Gurevitch. 1974. "Utilization of Mass Communication by the Individual." In *The Uses of Mass Communications: Current Perspectives on Gratifications Research*, eds. J. Blumer and E. Katz, 19–32. Beverly Hills, CA: Sage.

Katz, E., H. Haas, and M. Gurevitch. 1973. "On the Use of the Mass Media for Important Things." *American Sociological Review* 38, no. 2, pp. 164–81.

Keller, E.D. 2007. "Unleashing the Power of Word of Mouth: Creating Brand Advocacy to Drive Growth." *Journal of Advertising Research* 47, no. 4, pp. 448–52.

Kemp, S. January 8, 2014. "Social, Digital and Mobile in 2014." *We Are Social Singapore.* http://wearesocial.sg/blog/2014/01/social-digital-mobile-2014/

Kenneth, B. n.d. "What Is a Blog?" http://blogbasics.com/what-is-a-blog/

Kim, E.E.K., A.S. Mattila, and S. Baloglu. 2011. "Effects of Gender and Expertise on Consumers' Motivation to Read Online Hotel Reviews." *Cornell Hospitality Quarterly* 52, no. 4, pp. 399–406.

Kim, J., and P. Gupta. 2012. "Emotional Expressions in Online User Reviews: How They Influence Consumers' Product Evaluations." *Journal of Business Research* 65, no. 7, pp. 985–92.

King, D. August 26, 2011. "Wikipedia for Marketing, Should Your Business Use It?" www.socialfresh.com/wikipedia-marketing/

Klein, B.D. 1998. "Data Quality in the Practice of Consumer Product Management: Evidence from the Field." *Data Quality* 4, no. 1. pp. 19–40.

Koh. Y. July 1, 2010. "Japan, Champion at World Cup Tweeting." http://blogs.wsj.com/japanrealtime/2010/07/01/japan-champion-at-world-cup-tweeting/

Kokkoris, M.D., and U. Kühnen. 2015. "You Are (Not Only) What You Choose: A Self-Expression Account of Post-Choice Dissonance." *Motivation and Emotion* 39, no. 1, pp. 34–48.

Kopp, R. March 28, 2013. "Homegoroshi—Japanese Don't Always Like Positive Feedback." *Japan Intercultural Consulting.* http://japanintercultural.com/en/news/default.aspx?newsid=258

Kotler, P., N. Roberto, N., and N. Lee. 2002. *Social Marketing: Improving the Quality of Life.* 2nd ed. Thousand Oaks, CA: Sage Publications.

Kotler, P. 2012. *Kotler on Marketing.* New York, NY: Simon and Schuster.

Kozinets, R., A.C. Wojnicki, S.J. Wilner, and K. De Valck. 2010. "Networked Narratives: Understanding Word-of-Mouth Marketing in Online Communities." *Journal of Marketing* 74, no. 2, pp. 71–89.

Kraemer, K.L., J. Gibbs, and J. Dedrick. 2005. "Impacts of Globalization on E-Commerce Use and Firm Performance: A Cross-Country Investigation." *The Information Society* 21, no. 5, pp. 323–40.

Kumar, B. June 26, 2015. "5 Tips for Tapping into Your Buyer's Emotions with Content Marketing." www.leandatainc.com/uncategorized/5-tips-for-tapping-into-your-buyers-emotions-with-content-marketing

Lampe, C., N.B. Ellison, and C. Steinfield. November 2008. "Changes in Use and Perception of Facebook." In *Proceedings of the 2008 ACM Conference on Computer Supported Cooperative Work*, pp. 721–30. New York: ACM.

LaRose, R., and M.S. Eastin. 2004. "A Social Cognitive Theory of Internet Uses and Gratifications: Toward a New Model of Media Attendance." *Journal of Broadcasting and Electronic Media* 48, no. 3, pp. 358–77.

Lastowka, G. 2007. "User-Generated Content and Virtual Worlds." *Vanderbilt Journal of Entertainment and Technology Law* 10, p. 893.

Lee, J., D.H. Park, and I. Han. 2011. "The Different Effects of Online Consumer Reviews on Consumers' Purchase Intentions Depending on Trust in Online Shopping Malls: An Advertising Perspective." *Internet Research* 21, no. 2, pp. 187–206.

Lee, C.S., and L. Ma. 2012. "News Sharing in Social Media: The Effect of Gratifications and Prior Experience." *Computers in Human Behavior* 28, no. 2, pp. 331–39.

Leskovee, J., L. Adamic, and B. Huberman. 2007. "The Dynamics of Viral Marketing." *ACM TWeb* 1, no. 1.

Liang, T.P., H.J. Lai, and Y.C. Ku. 2006. "Personalized Content Recommendation and User Satisfaction: Theoretical Synthesis and Empirical Findings." *Journal of Management Information Systems* 23, no. 3, pp. 45–70.

Lim, Y., Y. Chung, and P.A. Weaver. 2012. "The Impact of Social Media on Destination Branding Consumer-Generated Videos Versus Destination Marketer-Generated Videos." *Journal of Vacation Marketing* 18, no. 3, pp. 197–206.

Litvin, S.W., R.E. Goldsmith, and B. Pan. 2008. "Electronic Word-of-Mouth in Hospitality and Tourism Management." *Tourism Management* 29, no. 3, pp. 458–68.

Liu, B.Q., and D.L. Goodhue. 2012. "Two Worlds of Trust for Potential E-Commerce Users: Humans as Cognitive Misers." *Information Systems Research* 23, no. 4, pp. 1246–62.

Lock, K. December 20, 2013. "Top 10 Image-Based Social Media Sites." www.webmaster.net/social-media/top-10-image-based-social-media-sites-0.html

Lohtia, R., N. Donthu, and E.K. Hershberger. 2003. "The Impact of Content and Design Elements on Banner Advertisement Clickthrough Rates." *Journal of Advertising Research* 50, no. 3, pp. 84–88.

Loureiro, S.M.C., and E. Kastenholz. 2011. "Corporate Reputation, Satisfaction, Delight, and Loyalty Towards Rural Lodging Units in Portugal." *International Journal of Hospitality Management* 30, no. 3, pp. 575–83.

Luca, M., and G. Zervas. 2013. *Fake It till You Make It: Reputation, Competition and Yelp Review Fraud.* Boston, MA: Harvard Business School.

Lusch, R.F., S.L. Vargo, and M. Tanniru. 2010. "Service, Value Networks and Learning." *Journal of the Academy of Marketing Science* 38, no. 1, pp. 19–31.

Mader, S. December 31, 2014. "7 Effective Wiki Uses and the Companies that Benefit from Them." http://stewartmader.com/7-effective-wiki-uses-and-the-companies-that-benefit-from-them/

Malaviya, P. July 2, 2013. "Consumer-Generated Ads: Good for Retention, Bad for Growth. Forbes." www.forbes.com/sites/onmarketing/2013/07/02/consumer-generated-ads-good-for-retention-bad-for-growth/

Malhotra, N.K., and J.D. McCort. 2001. "A Cross-Cultural Comparison of Behavioral Intention Models-Theoretical Consideration and an Empirical Investigation." *International Marketing Review* 18, no. 3, pp. 235–69.

Mangold, W.G., and D.J. Faulds. 2009. "Social Media: The New Hybrid Element of the Promotion Mix." *Business Horizons* 52, no. 4, pp. 357–65.

MarketingCharts Staff. January 15, 2015. "Social Logins in Q4: Google Gains on Facebook; LinkedIn Takes B2B Lead." www.marketingcharts.com/online/social-logins-in-q4-google-gains-on-facebook-linkedin-takes-b2b-lead-50502/

Mayzlin, D. 2006. "Promotional Chat on the Internet." *Marketing Science* 25, no. 2, pp. 155–63.

McDonald, S. 2010. "User-Generated Content and Future Challenges: New Kinds of Communication." *User Experience Magazine* 9, no. 4. Retrieved from http://uxpamagazine.org/new_kinds_of_communication/

McKenna, K.Y., and J.A. Bargh. 1999. "Causes and Consequences of Social Interaction on the Internet: A Conceptual Framework." *Media Psychology* 1, no. 3, pp. 249–69.

McKnight, D.H., L.L. Cummings, and N.L. Chervany. 1998. "Initial Trust Formation in New Organizational Relationships." *Academy of Management Review* 23, no. 3, pp. 473–90.

McMillan, D.W., and D.M. Chavis. 1986. "Sense of Community: A Definition and Theory." *Journal of Community Psychology* 14, no. 1, pp. 6–23.

McMillan, S.J. 2006. "Exploring Models of Interactivity from Multiple Research Traditions: Users, Documents, and Systems." *Handbook of New Media*, pp. 205–30.

McMillan, S.J., and M. Morrison. 2006. "Coming of Age with the Internet a Qualitative Exploration of How the Internet Has Become an Integral Part of Young People's Lives." *New Media and Society* 8, no. 1, pp. 73–95.

McQuail, D. 2000. *McQuail's Mass Communication Theory*. Sydney, Australia: Sage Publications.

Memcached. n.d. "What Is Memcached?" http://memcached.org/

Miller, N. 2007. "Manifesto for a New Age." *Wired* 15, no. 3, pp. 126–28.

Money, R.B., M.C. Gilly, and J.L. Graham. 1998. "Explorations of National Culture and Word-of-Mouth Referral Behavior in the Purchase of Industrial Services in the United States and Japan." *The Journal of Marketing*, pp. 76–87.

Moriuchi, E., and C. Chung. 2015. "The Factors that Affect Donation Advertising Effectiveness: An Experimental Research on Felt Ethnicity Towards In-Group and Out-Group from Young Americans' Perspectives." *Asia-Pacific Advances in Consumer Research* 11, pp. 206–7.

Moriuchi, E., and I. Takahashi. 2015. "An Empirical Investigation the Factors Motivating Japanese Repeat Online Consumers to Review Their Shopping Experience Online." *Proceedings from the Royal Bank International Research Seminar*. Montreal, Canada.

Mudambi, S.M., and D. Schuff. 2010. "What Makes a Helpful Review? A Study of Customer Reviews on Amazon.com." *MIS Quarterly* 34, no. 1, pp. 185–200.

Muñiz, A.M., and H.J. Schau. 2011. "How to Inspire Value-Laden Collaborative Consumer-Generated Content." *Business Horizons* 54, no. 3, pp. 209–17.

Murugesan, S. 2007. "Understanding Web 2.0." *IT Professional* 9, no. 4, pp. 34–41.

Mutum, D., and Q. Wang. 2010. "Consumer Generated Advertising in Blogs." In *Handbook of Research on Digital Media and Advertising: User Generated Content Consumption*, eds. M.S. Eastin, T. Daugherty and N.M. Burns, Vol. 1, pp. 248–61. Hershey, PA: IGI Global.

Nardi, B.A., D.J. Schiano, M. Gumbrecht, and L. Swartz. 2004. "Why We Blog." *Communications of the ACM* 47, no. 12, pp. 41–46.

Nathan, V. November 7, 2013. "Ten Ways Twitter's IPO Didn't Turn out to Be Like Facebook's IPO." www.forbes.com/sites/nathanvardi/2013/11/07/ten-ways-twitters-ipo-didnt-turn-out-to-be-like-facebooks-ipo/

Nielsen, J. April 17, 2006. "F-Shaped Pattern for Reading Web Content." www.nngroup.com/articles/f-shaped-pattern-reading-web-content/

Nielsen, J. October 9, 2006. "The 90-9-1 Rule for Participation Inequality in Social Media and Online Communities." www.nngroup.com/articles/participation-inequality/

Nielsen. April 10, 2012. "Nielsen Global Trust in Advertising and Brand Messages." www.nielsen.com/us/en/insights/reports/2012/global-trust-in-advertising-and-brand-messages.html

Nielsen. December 03, 2012. "Nielsen Social Media Report 2012: Social Media comes of Age." www.nielsen.com/us/en/insights/news/2012/social-media-report-2012-social-media-comes-of-age.html

Nielsen. February 2014. "The Digital Consumer." www.slideshare.net/tinhanhvy/the-digital-consumer-report-2014-nielsen?qid=310cce74-5ca8-4973-8b3e-28da9c4369e9&v=qf1&b=&from_search=3

Nielsen. May 2014. "Shifts in the Media Landscape." Nielsen Advertising and Audiences: State of the Media Report." www.nielsen.com/content/dam/nielsenglobal/jp/docs/report/2014/Nielsen_Advertising_and_%20 Audiences%20Report-FINAL.pdf

Nielsen Global Survey of Trust in Advertising. 2013. "Under the Influence: Consumer Trust in Advertising." www.nielsen.com/us/en/insights/news/2013/under-the-influence-consumer-trust-in-advertising.html

Nielsen Online. 2013. "Digital Influence: How the Internet Affects New Product Purchase Decisions." www.nielsen.com/us/en/insights/news/2013/digital-influence-how-the-internet-affects-new-product-purchase-decisions.html

Nishar, D. April 18, 2014. "The Next Three Billion [Infographic]." http://blog. linkedin.com/2014/04/18/the-next-three-billion/

O'Reilly, T. September 29, 2008. "Why Dell.com (was) More Enterprise 2.0 than Dell IdeaStorm." http://radar.oreilly.com/2008/09/why-dell-dot-com-is-more-enterprise.html

O'Keefe, D.J. 2003. "Message Properties, Mediating States, and Manipulation Checks: Claims, Evidence, and Data Analysis in Experimental Persuasive Message Effects Research." *Communication Theory* 13, no. 3, pp. 251–74.

O'Keefe, D.J., and J.D. Jensen. 2007. "The Relative Persuasiveness of Gain-Framed Loss-Framed Messages for Encouraging Disease Prevention Behaviors: A Meta-Analytic Review." *Journal of Health Communication* 12, no. 7, pp. 623–44.

Pan, B., T. MacLaurin, and J.C. Crotts. 2007. "Travel Blogs and the Implications for Destination Marketing." *Journal of Travel Research* 46, no. 1, pp. 35–45.

Papacharissi, Z., and A.M. Rubin. 2000. "Predictors of Internet Use." *Journal of Broadcasting and Electronic Media* 44, no. 2, pp. 175–96.

Papathanassis, A., and F. Knolle. 2011. "Exploring the Adoption and Processing of Online Holiday Reviews: A Grounded Theory Approach." *Tourism Management* 32, no. 2, pp. 215–24.

Park, C., and T.M. Lee. 2009. "Information Direction, Website Reputation and eWOM Effect: A Moderating Role of Product Type." *Journal of Business Research* 62, no. 1, pp. 61–67.

Park, D.H., and S. Kim. 2009. "The Effects of Consumer Knowledge on Message Processing of Electronic Word-of-Mouth via Online Consumer Reviews." *Electronic Commerce Research and Applications* 7, no. 4, pp. 399–410.

Park, D., J. Lee, and I. Han. 2007. "The Effect of On-Line Consumer Reviews on Consumer Purchase Intention: The Moderating Role of Involvement." *International Journal of Electronic Commerce* 11, no. 4, pp. 125–48.

Patel, N. April 15, 2015. "How to Write Content that Engages Mobile Readers." http://contentmarketinginstitute.com/2015/04/content-engages-mobile-readers/

Pavlou, P.A. 2003. "Consumer Acceptance of Electronic Commerce: Integrating Trust and Risk with the Technology Acceptance Model." *International Journal of Electronic Commerce* 7, no. 3, pp. 101–34.

Pavlou, P.A., and M. Fygenson. 2006. "Understanding and Predicting Electronic Commerce Adoption: An Extension of the Theory of Planned Behavior." *MIS Quarterly*, pp. 115–43.

PcMag. n.d. "Definition of Internet Forum." www.pcmag.com/encyclopedia/term/57794/internet-forum

Perry, D.K. 2002. *Theory and Research in Mass Communication: Contexts and Consequences.* 2nd ed. Mahwah, NJ: Lawrence Erlbaum Associates.

Petty, R.E., J.T. Cacioppo, and R. Goldman. 1981. "Personal Involvement as a Determinant of Argument-Based Persuasion." *Journal of Personality and Social Psychology* 41, no. 5, p. 847.

Petty, R.E., and J.T. Cacioppo. 1984. "The Effects of Involvement on Responses to Argument Quantity and Quality: Central and Peripheral Routes to Persuasion." *Journal of Personality and Social Psychology* 46, no. 1, p. 69.

Pew Internet Project's Research. n.d. "Social Networking Fact Sheet." www.pewinternet.org/fact-sheets/social-networking-fact-sheet/

Pew/Internet: Pew Internet and American Life Project. 2007. "Teens and Social Media: The Use of Social Media Gains a Greater Foothold in Teen Life as They Embrace the Conversational Nature of Interactive Online Media." www.pewinternet.org/files/old-media/Files/Reports/2007/PIP_Teens_Social_Media_Final.pdf.pdf

Pew Research Center. 2014. "Social Networking Fact Sheet: Highlights of the Pew Internet Project's Research Related to Social Networking." www.pewinternet.org/fact-sheets/social-networking-fact-sheet/

Plomion, B. 2014. "The 5 C's of Effective Content Marketing." www.convinceandconvert.com/content-marketing/the-5-cs-of-effective-content-marketing/

Pollach I. 2008. Electronic Word-of-Mouth: A Genre Approach to Consumer Communities." *International Journal of Web Based Communities Archive* 4, pp. 284–301.

Pookulangara, S., and K. Koesler. 2011. "Cultural Influence on Consumers' Usage of Social Networks and It's Impact on Online Purchase Intentions." *Journal of Retailing and Consumer Services* 18, no. 4, pp. 348–54.

Pornsakulvanich, V., P. Haridakis, and A.M. Rubin. 2008. "The Influence of Dispositions and Internet Motivation on Online Communication Satisfaction and Relationship Closeness." *Computers in Human Behavior* 24, no. 5, pp. 2292–310.

Preece, J. 2000. *Online Communities: Designing Usability and Supporting Sociability.* New York: John Wiley & Sons, Inc.

Preece, J., B. Nonnecke, and D. Andrews. 2004. "The Top Five Reasons for Lurking: Improving Community Experiences for Everyone." *Computers in Human Behavior* 20, no. 2, pp. 201–23.

Prentice, D.A., and D.T. Miller. 1992. "When Small Effects Are Impressive." *Psychological Bulletin* 112, no. 1, pp. 160–64.

Pulizzi, J. 2012. "The Rise of Storytelling as the New Marketing." *Publishing Research Quarterly* 28, no. 2, pp. 116–23.

Qualman, E. 2011. Social Media Revolution 2011. Social Media Revolution.

Qureshi, I., Y. Fang, E. Ramsey, P. McCole, P. Ibbotson, and D. Compeau. 2009. "Understanding Online Customer Repurchasing Intention and the Mediating Role of Trust–An Empirical Investigation in Two Developed Countries." *European Journal of Information Systems* 18, no. 3, pp. 205–22.

Rafaeli, S., and Y. Ariel. 2008. "11 Online Motivational Factors: Incentives for Participation and Contribution in Wikipedia." http://cdn.reclipper.com/0/5 89028a0c16016f869ce75d721659292.pdf

Rafaeli, S., and F. Sudweeks. 1997. "Networked Interactivity." *Journal of Computer-Mediated Communication* 2, no. 4.

Rainie, L., and B. Tancer. 2007. "Wikipedia: When in Doubt, Multitudes Seek It Out." Pew Internet and American Life Project. Washington, DC: Pew Research Center. www.pewinternet.org/2007/04/24/wikipedia-users/ (accessed October 12, 2007).

Read, D. 2007. "Experienced Utility: Utility Theory from Jeremy Bentham to Daniel Kahneman." *Thinking and Reasoning* 13, no. 1, pp. 45–61.

Resnick, P., R. Zeckhauser, E. Friedman, and K. Kuwabara. 2000. "Reputation Systems." *Communications of the ACM* 43, no. 12, pp. 45–48.

Retailing Today. July 12, 2013. "Study: 81% Research Online Before Making Big Purchases." *GE Capital Retail Bank Second Annual Report.* www.retailingtoday. com/article/study-81-research-online-making-big-purchases#

Revinate. 2011. "Information from Tripadvisors' Masterclass." http://blog. revinate.com/2011/04/information-from-tripadvisors-master-class.html

Rheingold, H. 2000. *Tools for Thought: The History and Future of Mind-Expanding Technology.* Cambridge, MA: MIT Press.

Roblyer, M.D., M. McDaniel, M. Webb, J. Herman, and J.V. Witty. 2010. "Findings on Facebook in Higher Education: A Comparison of College Faculty and Student Uses and Perceptions of Social Networking Sites." *The Internet and Higher Education* 13, no. 3, pp. 134–40.

Rodgers, S., E. Thorson, and Y. Jin. 2014. "Social Science Theories of Tradition and Internet Advertising." In *An Integrated Approach to Communication Theory and Research*, eds. D.W. Stacks and M.B. Salwen, 2nd ed. New York: Routledge.

Rogers Everett, M. 1983. *Diffusion of Innovations.* 3rd ed. New York: The Free Press.

Rogers, E.M. 1976. "New Product Adoption and Diffusion." *Journal of Consumer Research* 2, no, 4, pp. 290–301.

Ruchko, E. July 28, 2014. "8 Brands Effectively Leveraging User-Generated Content." www.tintup.com/blog/8-brands-effectively-leveraging-user-generated-content/

Ruggiero, T.E. 2000. "Uses and Gratifications Theory in the 21st Century." *Mass Communication and Society* 3, no. 1, pp. 3–37.

Rutledge, P. January 25, 2013. "How Obama Won the Social Media Battle in the 2012 Presidential Campaign." *The Media Psychology Blog*. http://mprcenter. org/blog/2013/01/how-obama-won-the-social-media-battle-in-the-2012-presidential-campaign/

Safko, J., and D.K. Brake. 2009. *The Social Media Bible*. Hoboken, NJ: John Wiley & Sons.

Saint, N. January 28, 2010. "What Is Foursquare and How Do I Use It?" www. businessinsider.com/how-hit-location-based-social-app-foursquare-works-2010-1?op=1

Sands, M. February 26, 2015. "How Marketers Can Make Data and Technology Work Better Together." www.iab.net/iablog/2015/02/how-marketers-can-make-data-and-technology-work-better-together.html#sthash.B8ICThJv.dpuf

Schindler, R.M., and B. Bickart. 2005. "Published Word of Mouth: Referable, Consumer-Generated Information on the Internet." *Online Consumer Psychology: Understanding and Influencing Consumer Behavior in the Virtual World*, pp. 35–61.

Scoble, R., and S. Israel. 2006. *Naked Conversations: How Blogs Are Changing the Way Businesses Talk with Customers*. Hoboken, NJ: John Wiley & Sons.

Sen, S., and D. Lerman. 2007. "Why Are You Telling Me This? An Examination into Negative Consumer Reviews on the Web." *Journal of Interactive Marketing* 21, no. 4, pp. 76–94.

Sengupta S. 2012. "Facebook Test: How to Please the New Faces." *New York Times*, May 15, A1.

Severin, W.J., and J.W. Tankard, Jr. 1992. *Communication Theories: Origins, Methods, and Uses in the Mass Media*. 3rd ed. White Plains, NY: Longman Publishing Group.

Shao, G. 2008. "Understanding the Appeal of User-Generated Media: A Uses and Gratifications Perspective." *Internet Research* 19, no. 1, pp. 72–75.

Shen, B., and K. Bissell. 2013. "Social Media, Social Me: A Content Analysis of Beauty Companies' Use of Facebook in Marketing and Branding." *Journal of Promotion Management* 19, no. 5, pp. 629–51.

Shiu, E. 2013. "Typical Innovative and Involvement Characteristics of Contributors to Consumer Generated Media." *Organizations and Social Networking: Utilizing Social Media to Engage Consumers*, pp. 103–24.

Sigala, M. 2008. "A Supply Chain Management Approach for Investigating the Role of Tour Operators on Sustainable Tourism: The Case of TUI." *Journal of Cleaner Production* 16, no. 15, pp. 1589–99.

Sigala, M., and O. Sakellaridis. 2004. "Web Users' Cultural Profiles and E-Service Quality: Internationalization Implications for Tourism Web Sites." *Information Technology and Tourism* 7, no. 1, pp. 13–22.

Smith, A. November 15, 2011. *Why Americans Use Social Media*. www.pewinternet.org/2011/11/15/why-americans-use-social-media/

Solomon, M.R., 2014. *Consumer Behavior: Buying, Having, and Being*. Upper Saddle River, NJ: Prentice Hall.

Sparks, B.A., and V. Browning. 2011. "The Impact of Online Reviews on Hotel Booking Intentions and Perception of Trust." *Tourism Management* 32, no. 6, pp. 1310–23.

Sparks, B.A., H.E. Perkins, and R. Buckley. 2013. "Online Travel Reviews as Persuasive Communication: The Effects of Content Type, Source, and Certification Logos on Consumer Behavior." *Tourism Management* 39, pp. 1–9.

Steffes, E.M., and L.E. Burgee. 2009. "Social Ties and Online Word of Mouth." *Internet Research* 19, no. 1, pp. 42–59.

Stern, B.B. 1994. "A Revised Communication Model for Advertising: Multiple Dimensions of the Source, the Message, and the Recipient." *Journal of Advertising* 23, no. 2, pp. 5–15.

Steyn, P., M.T. Ewing, G. Van Heerden, L.F. Pitt, and L. Windisch. 2011. "From Whence It Came: Understanding Source Effects in Consumer-Generated Advertising." *International Journal of Advertising* 30, no. 1, pp. 133–60.

Sun, T., Y. Seounmi, W. Guohua, and K. Mana. 2006. "Online Word-of-Mouth (or mouse): An Exploration of Its Antecedents and Consequences." *Journal of Computer-Mediated Communication* 11, no. 4, pp. 1104–27.

Sweeney, J.C., G.N. Soutar, and T. Mazzarol. 2008. "Factors Influencing Word of Mouth Effectiveness: Receiver Perspectives." *European Journal of Marketing* 42, no. 3/4, pp. 344–64.

Tajfel, H. 1982. "Social Psychology of Intergroup Relations." *Annual Review of Psychology* 33, no. 1, pp. 1–39.

Terdiman, D. December 15, 2005. "Study: Wikipedia as Accurate as Britannica." http://news.cnet.com/Study-Wikipedia-as-accurate-as-Britannica/2100-1038_3-5997332.html

The Digital Consumer. February 2014. "The Nielsen Company." www.slideshare.net/tinhanhvy/the-digital-consumer-report-2014-nielsen

Think with Google. June 2011. "Winning the Zero Moment of Truth-Ratings and Reviews: Word of MOT." www.thinkwithgoogle.com/interviews/winning-the-zero-moment-of-truth-ratings-and-reviews-word-of-mot.html

Thomson, S. November 2013. "What Brits Talk About and Where. Keller Fay Group." www.kellerfay.com/keller-fay-uk/brits-talk/

Tilton, S. February 15, 2012. "Coca-Cola's Content Strategy: Lessons for B2B Marketers." http://contentmarketinginstitute.com/2012/02/coca-colas-content-strategy-lessons-for-marketers/

Today. January 2014. "Facebook the Most Popular Social Network, Data Shows." www.todayonline.com/tech/facebook-most-popular-social-network-data-shows

Toh, R.S., C.F. DeKay, and P. Raven. 2011. "Travel Planning: Searching for and Booking Hotels on the Internet." *Cornell Hospitality Quarterly*, 52, no. 4, pp. 388–98. doi:1938965511418779

Trammell, K.D., and A. Keshelashvili. 2005. "Examining the New Influencers: A Self-Presentation Study of A-List Blogs." *Journalism and Mass Communication Quarterly* 82, no. 4, pp. 968–82.

Trepte, S. 2005. "Daily Talk as Self-Realization: An Empirical Study on Participation in Daily Talk Shows." *Media Psychology* 7, no. 2, pp. 165–89.

Triandis, H.C. 2001. "Individualism Collectivism and Personality." *Journal of Personality* 69, no. 6, pp. 907–24.

Triandis, H.C., and E.M. Suh. 2002. "Cultural Influences on Personality." *Annual Review of Psychology* 53, no. 1, pp. 133–60.

Tucker, T. 2011. "Online Word of Mouth: Characteristics of Yelp.com Reviews." *Elon Journal of Undergraduate Research in Communications* 2, pp. 37–42.

U.S. Census Bureau. 2012. "Measuring America: Computer and Internet Trends in America-Computer and Internet Use 1984-2012." www.census.gov/hhes/computer/files/2012/Computer_Use_Infographic_FINAL.pdf

U.S. Census Bureau News. November 17, 2015. "Quarterly Retail E-commerce Sales: 3rd Quarter 2015." www.census.gov/retail/mrts/www/data/pdf/ec_current.pdf

USA.gov: Government Made Easy. February 2, 2015. "What Is RSS? Everything You Need to Know to Subscribe to Government RSS Feeds." www.usa.gov/rss

Van Dijk, T.A. 2006. "Discourse, Context and Cognition." *Discourse Studies* 8, no. 1, pp. 159–77.

VanLear, C.A., M. Sheehan, L.A. Withers, and R.A. Walker. 2005. "AA Online: The Enactment of Supportive Computer Mediated Communication." *Western Journal of Communication* 69, no. 1, pp. 5–26.

Vargo, S.L. 2009. "Toward a Transcending Conceptualization of Relationship: A Service Dominant Logic Perspective." *Journal of Business and Industrial Marketing* 24, no. 5, pp. 373–78.

Vargo, S.L., and R.F. Lusch. 2004. "Evolving to a New Dominant Logic for Marketing." *Journal of Marketing* 68, no. 1, pp. 1–17.

Vermeulen, I.E., and D. Seegers. 2009. "Tried and Tested: The Impact of Online Hotel Reviews on Consumer Consideration." *Tourism Management* 30, no. 1, pp. 123–27.

Verna, P. June 2007. "User-Generated Content: Will Web 2.0 Pay Its Way?" *eMarketer*, 1–31.

Villi, M., J. Moisander, and A. Joy. 2012. "Social Curation in Consumer Communities: Consumers as Curators of Online Media Content." *Advances in Consumer Research* 40, pp. 490–95.

Vishwanath, A. 2004. "Manifestations of Interpersonal Trust in Online Interaction a Cross-Cultural Study Comparing the Differential Utilization of Seller Ratings by eBay Participants in Canada, France, and Germany." *New Media and Society* 6, no. 2, pp. 219–34.

Vivek, S.D., S.E. Beatty, and R.M. Morgan. 2012. "Customer Engagement: Exploring Customer Relationships Beyond Purchase." *Journal of Marketing Theory and Practice* 20, no. 2, pp. 122–46.

Vollmer, C., and G. Precourt. 2008. *Always on: Advertising, Marketing, and Media in an Era of Consumer Control.* New York: McGraw Hill Professional.

Wallace, P. 2001. *The Psychology of the Internet.* Cambridge, UK: Cambridge University Press.

Walther, J.B., B. Van Der Heide, L.M. Hamel, and H.C. Shulman. 2009. "Self-Generated Versus Other-Generated Statements and Impressions in Computer-Mediated Communication a Test of Warranting Theory Using Facebook." *Communication Research* 36, no. 2, pp. 229–53.

Wang, H.C., and H.S. Doong. 2010. "Argument form and Spokesperson Type: The Recommendation Strategy of Virtual Salespersons." *International Journal of Information Management* 30, no. 6, pp. 493–501.

Wang, H.-C., and M. Pomplun. 2012. "The Attraction of Visual Attention to Texts in Real-World Scenes." *Journal of Vision* 12, no. 6, p. 26. doi:10.1167/12.6.26

Wang, Y., and S. Rodgers. 2010. "Electronic Word of Mouth and Consumer Generated Content: From Concept to Application." In *Handbook of Research on Digital Media and Advertising: User Generated Content Consumption,* eds. M.S. Eastin, T. Daugherty, N.M Burns, 212–31. Hershey, PA: Information Science Reference.

Watts, S.A., and W. Zhang, 2008. "Capitalizing on Content: Information Adoption in Two Online Communities." *Journal of the Association for Information Systems* 9, no. 2, p. 3.

Weinberg, B.D., and E. Pehlivan. 2011. "Social Spending: Managing the Social Media Mix." *Business Horizons* 54, no. 3, pp. 275–82.

Westbrook, R.A., and R.L. Oliver. 1991. "The Dimensionality of Consumption Emotion Patterns and Consumer Satisfaction." *Journal of Consumer Research* 18, no. 1, pp. 84–91.

Whiting, A., and D. Williams. 2013. "Why People Use Social Media: A Uses and Gratifications Approach." *Qualitative Market Research: An International Journal* 16, no. 4, pp. 362–69.

Willemsen, L.M., P.C. Neijens, F. Bronner, and J.A. de Ridder. 2011. "'Highly Recommended!' The Content Characteristics and Perceived Usefulness of Online Consumer Reviews." *Journal of Computer-Mediated Communication* 17, no. 1, pp. 19–38.

Williams, D.L., V.L. Crittenden, T. Keo, and P. McCarty. 2012. "The Use of Social Media: An Exploratory Study of Usage Among Digital Natives." *Journal of Public Affairs* 12, no. 2, pp. 127–36.

Wilson, E.J., and D.L. Sherrell. 1993. "Source Effects in Communication and Persuasion Research: A Meta-Analysis of Effect Size." *Journal of the Academy of Marketing Science* 21, no. 2, pp. 101–12.

Witell, L., P. Kristensson, A. Gustafsson, and M. Löfgren. 2011. "Idea Generation: Customer Co-Creation Versus Traditional Market Research Techniques." *Journal of Service Management* 22, no. 2, pp. 140–59.

Wunsch-Vincent, S., and G. Vickery. 2006. *Participative Web: User-Created Content.* Paris: Organization for Economic Co-operation and Development.

Würtz, E. 2005. "Intercultural Communication on Web Sites: A Cross-Cultural Analysis of Web Sites from High-Context Cultures and Low-Context Cultures." *Journal of Computer-Mediated Communication* 11, no. 1, pp. 274–99.

Xia, L., and N.N. Bechwati. 2008. "Word of Mouse: The Role of Cognitive Personalization in Online Consumer Reviews." *Journal of Interactive Advertising* 9, no. 1, pp. 3–13.

Xiang, Z., and U. Gretzel. 2010. "Role of Social Media in Online Travel Information Search." *Tourism Management* 31, no. 2, pp. 179–88.

Xie, H.J., L. Miao, P.J. Kuo, and B.Y. Lee. 2011. "Consumers' Responses to Ambivalent Online Hotel Reviews: The Role of Perceived Source Credibility and Pre-Decisional Disposition." *International Journal of Hospitality Management* 30, no. 1, pp. 178–83.

Xifra, J., and A. Huertas. 2008. "Blogging PR: An Exploratory Analysis of Public Relations Weblogs." *Public Relations Review* 34, no. 3, pp. 269–75.

Yacouel, N., and A. Fleischer. 2012. "The Role of Cybermediaries in Reputation Building and Price Premiums in the Online Hotel Market." *Journal of Travel Research* 51, no. 2, pp. 219–26.

Ye, Q., R. Law, B. Gu, and W. Chen. 2011. "The Influence of User-Generated Content on Traveler Behavior: An Empirical Investigation on the Effects of E-Word-of-Mouth to Hotel Online Bookings." *Computers in Human Behavior* 27, no. 2, pp. 634–39.

Yi, Y., and T. Gong. 2013. "Customer Value Co-Creation Behavior: Scale Development and Validation." *Journal of Business Research* 66, no. 9, pp. 1279–84.

Yoo, K.H., and U. Gretzel. 2008. "What Motivates Consumers to Write Online Travel Reviews?" *Information Technology and Tourism* 10, no. 4, pp. 283–95.

Yoo, K.H., and U. Gretzel. 2011. "Influence of Personality on Travel-Related Consumer-Generated Media Creation." *Computers in Human Behavior* 27, no. 2, pp. 609–21.

Yoo, K.H., and U. Gretzel. 2012. "Use and Creation of Social Media by Travellers." *Social Media in Travel, Tourism and Hospitality: Theory, Practice and Cases*, p. 189.

Yousafzai, S.Y., G.R. Foxall, and J.G. Pallister. 2010. "Explaining Internet Banking Behavior: Theory of Reasoned Action, Theory of Planned Behavior, or Technology Acceptance Model?" *Journal of Applied Social Psychology* 40, no. 5, pp. 1172–202.

Zhu, F., and X. Zhang. 2006. "The Influence of Online Consumer Reviews on the Demand for Experience Goods: The Case of Video Games." *ICIS 2006 Proceedings*, p. 25.

Zhu, F., and X. Zhang. 2010. "Impact of Online Consumer Reviews on Sales: The Moderating Role of Product and Consumer Characteristics." *Journal of Marketing* 74, no. 2, pp. 133–48.

Index

OTHER TITLES IN DIGITAL AND SOCIAL MEDIA MARKETING AND ADVERTISING COLLECTION

Victoria L. Crittenden, Babson College, Editor

- *Social Content Marketing for Entrepreneurs* by James M. Barry
- *Digital Privacy in the Marketplace: Perspectives on the Information Exchange* by George Milne
- *This Note's For You: Popular Music + Advertising = Marketing Excellence* by David Allan
- *Digital Marketing Management: A Handbook for the Current (or Future) CEO* by Debra Zahay
- *Corporate Branding in Facebook Fan Pages: Ideas for Improving Your Brand Value* by Eliane Pereira Zamith Brito, Maria Carolina Zanette, Benjamin Rosenthal, Carla Caires Abdalla, and Mateus Ferreira
- *Presentation Skills: Educate, Inspire and Engage Your Audience* by Michael Weiss
- *The Connected Consumer* by Dinesh Kumar
- *Mobile Commerce: How It Contrasts, Challenges and Enhances Electronic Commerce* by Esther Swilley
- *Email Marketing in a Digital World: The Basics and Beyond* by Richard C. Hanna, Scott D. Swain and Jason Smith

Announcing the Business Expert Press Digital Library

Concise e-books business students need for classroom and research

This book can also be purchased in an e-book collection by your library as

- a one-time purchase,
- that is owned forever,
- allows for simultaneous readers,
- has no restrictions on printing, and
- can be downloaded as PDFs from within the library community.

Our digital library collections are a great solution to beat the rising cost of textbooks. E-books can be loaded into their course management systems or onto students' e-book readers.
The **Business Expert Press** digital libraries are very affordable, with no obligation to buy in future years. For more information, please visit **www.businessexpertpress.com/librarians**. To set up a trial in the United States, please email **sales@businessexpertpress.com**.

www.ingramcontent.com/pod-product-compliance
Lightning Source LLC
Chambersburg PA
CBHW062029200326
41519CB00017B/4979